ASHMOLEAN HANDBOOKS

English Embroideries of the Sixteenth and Seventeenth Centuries

in the collection of the
Ashmolean Museum

MARY M. BROOKS

Published in association with
Jonathan Horne Publications London
2004

ISBN 1 85444 192 2 (paperback)
ISBN 1 85444 193 0 (papercased)

Titles in this series include:
Ruskin's drawings
Worcester porcelain
Maiolica
Drawings by Michelangelo and Raphael
Oxford and the Pre-Raphaelites
Islamic ceramics
Indian paintings from Oxford collections
Camille Pissarro and his family
Eighteenth-century French porcelain
Miniatures
Samuel Palmer
Twentieth century paintings
Ancient Greek pottery
English Delftware
J.M.W. Turner
Glass of four millennia
Finger rings
Frames and framing
French drawings and watercolours
Scythian and Thracian antiquities

British Library Cataloguing in Publication Data
A catalogue record for this book is available from the British Library

Illustrations are reproduced by courtesy of the following: Bodleian Library p. 29, p. 33, p. 35, p. 45, p. 47, p.53; Rijskmuseum, Amsterdam, p. 37, p.63.

Cover illustration: *The Temptation of Adam and Eve*

Designed and typeset in Garamond and Frutiger by Rhian Lonergan-White, Ashmolean Museum.
Printed by Craft Print, Singapore

Contents

Key 17th-century events in England and dated Ashmolean Textiles

Political Events	Date	Dated embroideries in the Ashmolean
Accession of James VI of Scotland (James I of England) to the English throne on death of Elizabeth I	1603	
Accession of Charles I Marriage of Charles I to Henrietta Maria	1625	
Charles I embarked on 11 years of personal rule	1629	Embroidered picture, cat.3, *The Finding of Moses in the Nile*
Birth of the future Charles II	1630	
War with Scotland	1638	
Civil War	1641	
Charles I's Court at Oxford	1642	
Charles I surrendered to Scots. End of First Civil War	1646	
Second Civil War	1648	
Charles I executed; Commonwealth established under Cromwell	1649	
Charles II defeated; escaped to France	1651	
Cromwell designated Lord Protector	1653	
Protectorate parliament	1654	Embroidered picture, cat.11, *Ahasuerus & Esther* Initialled A H
Act for discovering, converting & repressing of Popish Recusants	1656	
Cromwell offered and refused Kingship; drew up new constitution	1657	
Cromwell died. Richard Cromwell, his son, succeeded. Parliament recalled by Army after Richard forced from power	1658	
Charles II restored to throne	1660 1661	Sampler Mary Parker Embroidered picture, cat.8, *David & Bathsheba* Initialled S C Date unclear; could be 1661 or 1681

Political Events	Date	Dated embroideries in the Ashmolean
Marriage of Charles II to Catherine of Braganza	1662	
Great Plague of London	1665	Embroidered box with *Scenes from the life of Abraham*, cat.7, made after the Plague, possibly by Miss Bluitt, later Mrs Payne
Great Fire of London	1666	
	1667	Sampler Suzannah Connington, cat.16
Test Act (excluded Roman Catholics from public office)	1673	Embroidered picture, cat.6, *The Sacrifice of Isaac* Date unclear, probably 1673 Initialled I (E or Y)
Marriage of Princess Mary (daughter of future James II and niece of Charles II) to William III of Orange	1677	
Accession of James II	1685	
William of Orange invades England; James II flees to France	1688	
James II's flight declared to be an act of abdication. William and Mary invited to become joint rulers. Bill of Rights passed	1689	
Death of Mary	1694	
	1699	Sampler Mary Parker, cat.16
Accession of Anne (daughter of James II and niece of Charles II)	1702	
Act of Union between Scotland and England	1707	

Rulers in 17th-century England

James I of England & VI of Scotland
married Anne of Denmark
- Born 1566
- Succeeded 1603
- Died 1625

Henry, Prince of Wales
- Born 1594
- Died 1612

Elizabeth married Frederick of the Palatine
- Born 1596
- Died 1662

Charles I married Henrietta Maria of France
- Born 1600
- Succeeded 1625
- Executed by order of Parliament 30 Jan 1649

Commonwealth & Protectorate

Oliver Cromwell Lord Protector
- Born 1599
- Head of Comonwealth 1649–1653
- Lord Protector 1653–1658
- Died 1658

Richard Cromwell Lord Protector
- Born 1626
- Lord Protector 1658–1659
- Died 1712

Charles II married Catherine of Braganza
- Born 1630
- Proclaimed King in Scotland 1649
- Restoration of monarchy in England 1660
- Died 1685

Anne Hyde married (1) 1660

James II
- Born 1633
- Succeeded 1685
- Deposed 1688
- Died 1701

Mary married **William III of Orange**
- Born 1662
- Proclaimed King & Queen 1689
- Died 1694
- Born 1650
- Died 1702

Anne
- Born 1665
- Succeeded 1702
- Died 1714

6

English Embroideries: Collectors, Makers and Sources

The Ashmolean Museum contains a small but high quality collection of English sixteenth- and seventeenth-century embroideries including pictorial panels, a box, samplers, costume items and some fanciful novelty pieces. The pictorial panels depict biblical, classical or allegorical themes and have an immediate appeal. They create miniature, often three-dimensional, worlds peopled with kings and queens, heroes and fashionable ladies and gentlemen set in landscapes filled with animals and flowers; they are worked in colourful silk and glinting metal threads. The samplers demonstrate the importance of the development of girls' embroidery skills while the carefully balanced floral motifs on the costume pieces show the application of such patterns and stitches.

At a conservative estimate, at least a thousand of these pictorial embroideries survive. They were usually made by well-off schoolgirls and young women who had both the luxury of time and the financial resources to purchase expensive fabrics, threads, sequins and semi-precious stones. The embroideries were made during one of the most turbulent centuries in English history, when religious and political beliefs split families and the country. Crises over the succession of power followed one after another. The execution of Charles I, the failure of Parliamentary rule to sustain itself after Oliver Cromwell's death, and the lack of a legitimate Protestant heir to Charles II all dramatically focused attention on issues of dynasty and inheritance. Paradoxically these embroideries often depict biblical stories at a time when religious issues, including the use of images, aroused great controversy. The long journey travelled by such images from the original artist to the embroiderer is complex and requires careful consideration. During a period of increasing urbanisation, the pictorial pieces often show idyllic country scenes. Despite depicting imaginary creatures and flowers, the embroideries also show fashionable clothing and ceremonial textiles. Exploring the use that artists and poets made of the themes which appear on the embroideries may provide insights into why certain stories were popular and what their possible contemporary significance may have been, beyond that of providing an opportunity for displaying technical ability. The role that these embroideries played in both creating and reflecting ideals of feminine behaviour is also an important part of their history.

The Collectors of English Sixteenth- & Seventeenth-Century Embroideries

Western collectors have tended to value the fine arts, such as painting and sculpture, over the decorative arts such as furniture, metalwork and textiles and to prefer pieces which can be identified with specific artists or artistic traditions. These embroideries do not fit these categories so that the growth of interest in their collection and study is an interesting phenomenon in itself. Their contemporaries appear to have considered them as schoolgirl work or as personal feminine possessions that did not justify financial valuation as they rarely appear in inventories or wills. Collectors were slow to pay them serious attention and they were often dismissed as crude and unskilled work. As late as 1961, one embroidery historian described them as 'schoolgirl gaucheries', lacking 'any idea of grace or style'. Nevertheless, around the turn of the twentieth century, their status altered dramatically. They moved from being domestic pieces, saved, like the Ashmolean box, out of family loyalty, to becoming highly desirable objects, collected by wealthy, often male, connoisseurs. Interest in these embroideries increased to the extent that 'replicas' were made. These have sometimes entered collections as genuine examples.

The pioneer collections were well established by the early twentieth century. Sir Frank Richmond began collecting in the 1910s. He was Director of Debenham's, a leading London store, and set up a department selling Tudor and Stuart embroideries. Other shops such as Jenner's in Edinburgh and Wiley & Lockhead in Glasgow followed suit. Charity exhibitions became fashionable as part of London's social scene. The 1928 *Exhibition of Early English Needlework & Furniture* was organised in aid of the Royal Northern Hospital while J. Francis Mallett donated the entry fees from exhibitions at his Bond Street shop to the National Art Collections Fund. By the 1930s, *The Connoisseur, Apollo* and *Old Furniture* were regularly publishing articles on seventeenth-century embroidery. The Victoria & Albert Museum's catalogue of sixteenth- and seventeenth-century embroideries was first published in 1938, a significant indicator of increasing scholarship. Collections owned by important connoisseurs such as Sir Percival Griffiths were sold at auction, reinforcing the financial value of the embroideries as well as their aesthetic and historical importance. Lord Leverhulme's collecting instinct differed from that of many of the other connoisseurs. As well as purchasing for his own collection, he was buying embroideries for public exhibition, eventually at Port Sunlight, Liverpool. Inspired by the ideals of the Arts and Crafts movement, he wanted to place the 'Art of the home … within the reach of all of us, however humble…'. Others were anxious to ensure that textiles had the same status as the other decorative arts. Judge Irwin Untermyer, an American collector, was clear about the importance of his collection:

> It is not presumptuous to say … that such a collection can probably not be formed again for, in recent years, some needlework pictures of fine quality, condition and important size have passed into museums' collections.

This comment neatly pinpoints a transitional moment in the status of these embroideries. Having left the family domain, they were moving from the commercial arena into the museum world. This gave them status and value while simultaneously removing them from the scope of private collectors. Judge Untermyer seemed to be particularly attracted by their 'Englishness':

> The charm is enhanced by an unconscious defiance of the laws of nature, the sun and the moon resplendent at the same time and the lion, the leopard and the tiger fraternizing with mankind against the background of an English mansion in an English countryside watered by an English stream.

This paradisical vision may also have been an attraction for early twentieth-century English collectors as the country struggled to re-establish a sense of identity and purpose after the First World War.

The Mallett Donation

In 1947, J. Francis Mallett, a noted connoisseur, made an extremely generous bequest to the Ashmolean Museum. Born John Francis Snook, he changed his name when he married Margaret Mallett, the daughter of Walter Mallett who ran an antique and jewellery business in Bath. The firm developed expertise in furniture and decorative arts and opened a large London showroom. Mallett's legacy of his personal collection of ceramics, miniatures, furniture, clocks, silver, and enamels was described by the Keeper, Karl Parker, as 'one of the most munificent bequests we have ever received'. A gallery at the Ashmolean was named in Mallett's honour and his daughter Elizabeth continued the link with the museum, making several donations.

John Francis Mallett

Mallett's bequest includes pictorial panels, most showing Old Testament scenes, two samplers, some small costume items and fanciful pieces such as a frog-shaped purse, a tape measure made from a nut and three flower 'favours'. The embroideries illustrate most of the usual techniques for the period with the notable exception of beadwork. Two techniques dominate: either flat stitches which create smooth, sometimes glossy, surfaces or inventive raised work. This often involved the use of sections of separately worked detached needlepoint lace, wired or padded to create miniature sculptural forms. This distinctive, peculiarly English, type of embroidery was christened 'stump work' by later textile historians but at the time was apparently called 'raised' or 'embossed' work.

Such pictorial embroideries often combine different biblical or classical stories on one piece. However, the majority of Mallett's pieces have very focused designs and only occasionally feature symbolic motifs. This is unusual and seems to suggest that Mallett preferred single narrative biblical embroideries. It also highlights the significance of the more unusual symbolic motifs when they do appear. It is worth noting that Mallett's collection does not contain embroideries which are 'portraits' of individuals or showing couples, both common at this period. Nor does it include examples of embroideries depicting the popular stories of the triumphant Old Testament heroines Judith, Jael or Deborah, all women who displayed courage, indeed outright violence, in defence of their people. Collectors themselves can thus influence our awareness of key themes.

The collection has been enriched by later donors, notably John Buxton, a poet, writer and naturalist who was a Fellow of New College, Oxford. His 1990 bequest includes a late sixteenth- or early seventeenth-century embroidery of a deer, doe and flowering tree, initialled A M, a sadly faded seventeenth-century embroidery of *The Sacrifice of Isaac*, a late seventeenth-century woman's waistcoat and an eighteenth-century stomacher.

The Makers

Professional embroiderers were normally men working within the established framework of the guilds which aimed to control entry to the trades and were supposed to maintain standards. The small embroidery showing a vase with flowers and lively insects, donated by A.G.B. Russell (cat.22), is likely to be professional work. Such work does not seem to have been of great interest to Mallett. The single such piece in his bequest is probably the pair of glove gauntlets (cat.17) and most of the embroideries in his gift were made by schoolgirls or young women. This does not mean that the standard of work could not reach extraordinary levels of skill and intricacy. Martha Edlin's embroidered boxes, samplers, needlework accessories and miniatures from the 1670s have, amazingly, all survived together and are now in the Victoria & Albert Museum. Martha made these pieces between the ages of eight and thirteen and they clearly demonstrate the range of techniques and technical skill which girls were able to achieve.

There were periodic – and often raucous – pamphlet wars in the seventeenth century over the status and role of women. A married woman was under her husband's financial and legal control. For most women, marriage was the central defining experience of their lives and was crucial in securing their economic and social status. Despite some radical explorations of women's position, the Civil War probably had the greatest impact on women's lives. Both Royalist and Parliamentary women were involved in the realities of war, physically defending their homes and towns or undertaking legal petitions to reclaim their husbands' property.

The debate over women's education needs to be seen within in this changing context. Although reformers such as Mary Astell sought to establish women's right to a serious education in order 'to furnish our minds with a stock of useful knowledge that the Souls of Women may no longer be unadorn'd and neglected things', needlework was seen as a primary means of demonstrating feminine qualities. Note the order in which Evelyn lists the qualities possessed by his daughter Susanna:

> She is a good Child, religious, discreete, Ingenious, and qualified with all the ornaments of her sex: especially has a peculiar talent in Designe and Painting both in oyle and Miniature, and with a genious extraordinary, for whatever hands can pretend to do with the Needle: Has the French Toung, has read most of the Greek and Roman Authors, Poets, using her talents with great Modesty, Exquisitely shap'd, and of an agreeable Countenance…

Although Evelyn certainly appreciated educated women, Susanna's skills at painting and needlework take precedence over her linguistic skills and literary understanding. The memorial verses for Susanna Perwich, who taught in her mother's boarding school before her early death in 1661, praised her skill in embroidering 'Pictures of men, birds, beasts & flowers' although she was also trained in music, mathematics and calligraphy. Others had no hesitation in openly stating that there was little point in female education. One member of the Vernon family put it bluntly: 'and being a girl she shall not learn latin, so she will have more time for breeding hereafter and needlework to.'

Nevertheless, many girls did attend school although the curriculum tended to be geared as much towards the attainment of socially acceptable skills as to intellectual achievement. In 1628, the Court of Aldermen paid £21 a year for Anne Heather, an orphan ward, to attend Mrs Friend's school in Stepney where she was taught 'learning at her needle, writing, musick and other qualities'. Hackney, also situated outside London where the air was thought to be healthier, had so many schools it became known as 'The Ladies University of the Female Arts'. In 1667, Pepys attended Hackney Church specifically 'to see the young ladies of the schools, whereof there is great store, very pretty'. These schools were not small concerns. During the Civil War and Commonwealth years, over 800 girls passed through Mrs Perwich's Hackney school. It seems likely that many of the surviving embroideries were made at such schools. In 1639, Susan Nicholas's school bills included the cost of materials which seem to be for an embroidery project:

cat.7 detail, Isaac and Rebecca

For watchett sattin for her Sweet Bag	4 shillings	6 pence
For Taffetie	13 shillings	
For Gold & Silver Lace	18 shillings	10 pence
For Silver Ribbin	2 shillings	3 pence
For an ounce of Silver Thread	5 shillings	4 pence

This compares with a weekly payment of 8 pence for laundry. The intriguing note preserved with the Ashmolean's box (cat.7) provides a rare link between an embroiderer and her school:

> The cabinet was made by my Mother's Grandmother who was educated at Hackney School after the Plague in London all the young Ladies works were ~~burnt~~ (sic) destroyed that they were about at that time, she left school soon after, therefore this was made that vis before 1665…

Clearly, the girls' needlework was thought to have the potential to transmit plague and was therefore destroyed as a safety measure.

The cost of acquiring these socially desirable feminine skills was considerable. The Earl of Thomond's daughters had needlework lessons at home from Mrs Hannah Senior who was paid £20 a year. Sir Edmund Verney was quite explicit about his motivation when he agreed to his daughter Mary's request for money to learn a new handicraft at school: 'I approve of it … for I admire all accomplishments that will render you considerable and Lovely in the sight of God and man…'.

His investment could bring both social and religious rewards. Hannah Woolley made an explicit link between needlework and moral behaviour in her 1688 conduct book *A Guide to Ladies, Gentlewomen & Maids*. In her multiple careers of governess, school mistress and author, she capitalised on her own embroidery skills and argued that needlework: 'is both needfull and pleasant, and is commendable in any woman, for it is time well spent for both profit and delight.'

It also gave servants a gainful occupation: 'A due calling of the Maiden-servants to the Needle on an Afternoon, such as else would be idle, and giggling with the fellows.'

Hannah Woolley seems to have been a strict mentor, admonishing girls to do their work:

> well, though you do the less, and do not waste your silke or thread …do not loss (sic) your Needles nor break them willingly to be idle. Sit upright at your work, and do not lean nor loll for that will make you crooked.

Servants and poor girls were not taught the 'curious' (fancy) work learnt by well-off schoolgirls. Their training, like that of Mary Tristram, who was apprenticed to Mrs Susan Beeke in 1626 'for sempstress work and other things belonging to a servant maid', focused on 'plain' (utilitarian) needlework.

Although the schools were often associated with religious dissenters, they had critics. Some considered their curriculum frivolous and Aubrey condemned them as places where girls learnt 'pride and wantonness'. Conscientious Puritan mothers such as Elizabeth Walker taught their children at home, 'not to save Charges' but to 'keep their Minds uncorrupted by Vanity or Pride'. In contrast to Hannah Woolley's argument that needlework was improving and a good use of time, Elizabeth Walker viewed needlework as self-indulgence, a distraction from her duty:

> 'she was Mistress of her needle to that degree, that she would blame herself that she had spent so much time and industry, to attain it in worsted, silk and finest Thread…'

Some girls had strong feelings about their rigorous needlework education. Anne D'Ewes noted her niece did not want to return to school because she so disliked embroidery 'that she cries almost every day…'. Lucy Hutchinson's biography of her husband describes her own early life. She is crystal clear about her attitude: 'and for my needle, I absolutely hated it.'

From Print to Textile

Many of the biblical embroideries derive from Continental designs. These, and other printed sources, became increasingly available during the seventeenth century. Peter Stent was a well-known London print seller. His 1653 and 1662 advertisements listing 'Books, Pictures and Maps' include illustrated copybooks, political portraits and biblical prints such as *Adam and Eve* and *Abraham offering Isak.*

Gerard de Jode's 1585 *Thesaurus Sacrarum Historiarum Veteris Testamenti* tells the Old Testament story through elegant engravings by different artists and was a popular design source for wallpaintings, silver and plasterwork as well as textiles. Bernard Salomon's less sophisticated illustrations to Claude Paradin's 1553 Bible picture book, *Quadrins Historique de la Bible,* were also frequently used. Similarities between some embroideries, such as the Ashmolean's *Ahasuerus and Esther* (cat.11) and the almost identical piece in the Burrell Collection, Glasgow, are due to more than just a common print source. The way in which the source prints have been modified and combined with stock motifs suggests the involvement of intermediaries. These are possibly the pattern drawers who seem to have been involved in the process of transferring the image from print to fabric. There is generally less correspondence than might be expected than if the designs were being prepared for sale in a completely standardised manner. This seems to indicate that the embroiderer – or her teacher – could exercise choice in the selection and combination of images. The 1607 play *The Faire Maide of the Exchange* features an unnamed cripple who works as a pattern drawer at the Royal Exchange, an important centre for shopping in London. Phillis, the sweet but self-willed heroine, gives precise instructions about the images she wants drawn on a handkerchief so she can embroider a covert message of love to the hero Frank:

> Here is bespoke worke which must be wrought
> With expedition …
> In one corner of the same, place wanton loue,
> Drawing his bow shooting an amorous dart,
> Opposite against him an arrow in a heart,
> In a third corner picture foorth disdaine,
> A cruell fate unto a louing vaine.
> In the fourth drawe a springing Lawrell tree,
> Circled about with a ring of poesie…

Frustratingly, no clues are given about the pattern drawer's equipment or methods.

Not all embroiderers used printed sources or the services of a pattern drawer. Drawing one's own design was always an option. Grace Sherrington Laycock's evident pride in her own design work suggests this was unusual: '…every day I spent some tyme in works of myne owne invention, without sample or pattern before me and to drawe flowers and fruitt to their lyfe with my plumett upon paper.'

Others had designs created specifically. Mary, Duchess of Bedford, was a skilled embroiderer who was also a respected plantswoman. She arranged for her footman Daniel Francom to learn painting so he could create images for her embroidery, noting that: 'He has made a shift to paint some Aloes. I intend to send it to London to be drawn upon canvas …I will work it for a screen.' Interestingly, this implies the involvement of professionals to scale the image up for embroidery. Shorleyker's 1624 pattern book *A Schole-house for the Needle* usefully included a grid to 'contrive any worke, Bird, Beast, or Flower into bigger or lesser proportions.' One surviving copy shows evidence of the 'prick and pounce' method of transferring images. Small holes were 'pricked' in the paper and charcoal rubbed through to transfer the design to the fabric. This preserves the scale of the printed design and may account for the incongruities in size, which do not appear to have disconcerted the embroiderers. Unfinished or degraded embroideries clearly show inked designs, occasionally with coloured highlights. Sometimes, as with the children's faces on the Ashmolean's *Charity* (cat.14), it seems that parts of the design were intended to remain unembroidered.

Images and Meaning

These methods of transferring designs create some distance between the embroiderer and the image. Seeing the design as an expression of personal feelings may not be valid. If the embroiderer – or teacher – was selecting from a predetermined range of images, did they have any religious, political or personal meaning for her or did they reflect wider interests and concerns? It is hard to establish how much the significance of the image changed as it passed from the original artist through, possibly, the printmaker, print seller, pattern drawer and teacher to the embroiderer. It is must always be remembered that the embroiderer could have selected the subject for the opportunity it offered to display her skills rather than seeking to create an embroidery with overt or cryptic symbolic meanings.

At one point, it was thought that all the motifs had symbolic significance. Common motifs such as caterpillars and butterflies have been interpreted as symbolising, respectively, Charles I and the Restoration. Mallett suggested the following interpretations:

> a lion (strength), a stag (divine influence), a dog (fidelity), a parrot or snail (wisdom), silk worm (industry), a butterfly (joy), a snail (patience), hen & chickens (divine protection & maternal love).

Some embroiderers clearly did intend a symbolic meaning but additional information is necessary to clarify this. Hannah Smith was in Royalist Oxford in 1656 when she completed her embroidered box, now in the Whitworth Gallery, Manchester. A political, probably Royalist, reading of the story of *Joseph in the Pit* is reinforced by the recent discovery of a crowned head, cunningly concealed within the embroidery. Damaris Pearse's unusual embroidery of *The Drowning of Pharaoh in the Red Sea* is now in the Lady Lever Art Gallery,

Liverpool. Her father published a book commemorating her short life which provides information on her Protestant background, thus supporting a religious-political reading. Such contextual information is highly unusual. Sometimes, an unusual image or a combination of narrative theme and image suggests a specific religious or political affiliation on the part of the embroiderer, her teacher, her family or the pattern drawer, but great caution is required in drawing any firm conclusions.

Biblical Themes

The seventeenth century's expertise with biblical interpretation enabled Old Testament images to be seen both as foreshadowing New Testament stories and as bearing contemporaneous political or social meanings. Biblical stories such as those of Eve, Sarah, Hagar and Esther were clearly related to ideas about women's obedience, marriage, and the birth of heirs. Their use by artists and poets can illuminate their possible meanings for the embroiderers.

The story of Moses focuses attention on the importance of male children and attracted several early seventeenth-century painters. Charles I owned one version of Orazio Gentileschi's painting *The Finding of Moses*. This may refer to the birth of the Prince of Wales in 1630, comparing his birth as the royal heir, securing the Stuart succession, with the birth of Moses, the saviour of the Israelites. This royal link is further reinforced by the Stuart claim of descent from Pharaoh's daughter, based on the unlikely argument that she was named 'Scota'. Charles II's interest in this theme is suggested by his commissioning Jacob de Wet's painting *The Finding of Moses* for his closet in Holyrood Castle, Edinburgh. There is some evidence that suggests he saw himself as a Moses-like figure who had delivered his people through the restoration of the monarchy. The heroic figure of Moses as deliverer could be claimed by both royalists and parliamentarians. Damaris Pearse's father discusses his daughter's embroidery of *The Drowning of Pharaoh* and makes an explicit link between Cromwell and Moses.

The story of Abraham and his extended family had tremendous religious and political resonance and was one of the most popular embroidery themes. As the founder of the Hebrew nation, Abraham was a model for kings. Henry VIII, like many other rulers, drew parallels between Abraham's dynasty and the Tudor line. The famous Abraham tapestries, now at Hampton Court Palace, explicitly set up comparisons between Abraham and his heir Isaac with Henry and his heir Edward. These tapestries were retained under the Commonwealth for Cromwell's use, suggesting that they were important not only for their extraordinary financial value but also for the significance of the message they conveyed about inheritance and succession. The Protectorate government commissioned a new cycle of Abraham tapestries from the Mortlake tapestry factory in 1657, reinforcing this argument. Abraham also represented unconditional obedient faith in God through his willing sacrifice of Isaac, foreshadowing God's sacrifice of Christ, his own son. For the schoolgirl embroidering scenes from the life of Abraham, the significance could have been the stories of Sarah, Hagar and Rebecca. These all offer reflections on the importance of marriage, heirs and the proper behaviour of women. Sarah was held up as a role model by N H in *The Ladies Dictionary* (1690) which presented 'the whole Series and Order, of all the most Herrick (heroic) and Illustrious, Women of all times'. In her private notebook, Elizabeth Walker quoted Peter, who held Sarah up as the example of an ideal wife: 'Likewise, ye Wives be in subjection to your own Husbands, even as Sarah obeyed Abraham, calling him Lord.' (1 Peter 3: 6.)

The theme of an adulterous liaison and a murder appears to be an unlikely subject for young girls but the story of David and Bathsheba was presented as moral tale. The anonymous poet who wrote *David's Troubles Remembered* (1638) attempted the delicate task of making Bathsheba both virtuous and alluring:

> Sweet Bathsheba, Judeas fairest Maid .....
> Wife modest, valiant and religious
> Was ever Virgin to the Temple led
> More chaste than she unto Uriah's bed?......

David is presented as an innocent corrupted:

> Lo he whose soul was like a weaned Child
> Pure, simple, abstinent, and undefil'd
> Becomes impure, thus is base slime and dust
> From heavenly thoughts proclive to fleeting lust ...

> But as you evermore shall see one sinne
> Beget another, to lye hidden in,
> So David, his Adultery to hide,
> Commits first drunkenness, then homicide ....

N H in *The Ladies Dictionary* is in no doubt that the fault lay initially in Bathsheba's immodest exposure:

> ... her naked beauties so Inchanted King David, who espyed her from a Turras, as she was washing in a Fountain; that he procured her Husband to be slain, and took her to Wife.... That Prince was holy, and Bathsheba on whom by accident he cast his Eyes, was innocent, but she was naked: David saw her in that posture, and there needed no more to make David loose his Holinesse and Bathsheba her Innocence.

Despite advice given elsewhere on beautification, N H draws the moral regarding women's behaviour: 'We find by lamentable, if I may not say, fatal Experience, that the world to much allows nakedness in women.'

Bathsheba is depicted as a warning to girls about appropriate behaviour although the drama of the story and lure of attractive images, often based on engravings from Gerard de Jode's collection, was probably also a factor in the frequency with which it was selected for embroidery.

The story of Esther also had strong appeal. The Duke of Buckingham hung Veronese's *King Ahasuerus and Queen Hester* (sic) in the King's Bed Chamber in York House in 1635. Henry Percy's 1632–33 probate inventory lists 'six peeces of hanginges' showing the story. Contemporary references make it clear that, as well as being a female role model, Esther's bold intercession on behalf of her people could be used to support different political positions. The 1617 pamphlet *Ester hath hang'd Haman*, probably written by a woman under the pseudonym 'Ester Sowernam', uses the story to justify female defiance. In contrast, Hannibal Gamon's 1627 funeral sermon for Lady Robartes praises her dutiful obedience by comparing her with Esther:

cat.11, detail of lion with bone

> … there are more … proud Vastby's [Vashti, Ahasuerus's first wife, dismissed for disobedience] than humble Esthers … How shall she [Lady Robartes] be Praised in respect of her Parents? …. as Esther, who did the Commandement of Mordecay when she was a Queene and procured the Enlargement and Deliverance of her kindred with her Feasts, her Teares, and the Hazard of her Life.

At least thirty embroideries showing the story of Esther survive, drawing on different print sources. Several follow an engraving by the Netherlandish artist Martin van Heemskerk while others, including the Ashmolean's example, draw on the Gerard de Jode engraving. The close similarities between 1652 version in the Burrell Collection, Glasgow and the 1654 version in the Ashmolean are intriguing (cat.11). Both were worked during the Cromwellian period and share many of the same design features, although there are significant differences. In the Burrell embroidery, the lion sits before a pile of clean bones while the lion in the Ashmolean piece has a bloody bone in his mouth. The rainbow and fountain, topped with Old Father Time carrying a host (communion wafer) in a winged chalice only appear in the Ashmolean piece. The very rarity of the image of the lion, particularly in combination with the highly unusual fountain design, suggests a political or religious meaning is intended.

Solomon was seen as the model of a wise king, bringing peace and prosperity. Both Henry VIII and James I & VI repeatedly identified themselves with him. The Ashmolean's unusual embroidery *The Proclamation of Solomon* (cat.9) focuses on the moment of the confirmation of Solomon's kingship, and thus points to issues of the continuity of monarchy and power. This embroidery could be seen as conservative, supporting the divine descent of kings, or radical, suggesting that rulers could be created by proclamation. Other motifs do little to clarify the position. The lion and leopard could be Royalist symbols. However, these motifs could equally have been selected purely for their decorative value, particularly given the presence of the delightful mermaid. No direct print source has been identified for the Ashmolean's embroidery showing *Solomon and the Queen of Sheba* (cat.10). Sheba's visit to Solomon could be viewed as a model for the relationship of Christ and the Church or for the ideal marriage, linking wisdom and wealth. The embroidery could thus be a compliment to the monarch, particularly if Solomon is shown with Stuart features, or refer to more personal issues, such as marriage. However, caution must be exercised with such readings. The mermaid, animals and flowers suggest that this is a compendium of images which may combine political, religious or moral reflections with the sheer enjoyment of an exuberant embroidery technique executed with great skill and aplomb.

Symbolic Motifs & Repeating Patterns

The comparative rarity of symbolic motifs in the embroideries in Mallett's collection has already been noted. The appearance of the emblematic obelisks in the border of *The Finding of Moses* (cat.3) is therefore doubly interesting. These obelisks, wound around with a twining plant, derive from Whitney's 1586 book *A Choice of Emblems*. Each image is accompanied with a verse, creating a fusion of textual and visual meaning. Whitney modified the verse for the obelisk image to form a compliment to Elizabeth I but the image could equally well refer to dynastic, religious or personal faithfulness and so would be appropriate for the marriage theme suggested by the twinned coats of arms:

cat.3, detail of obelisk

> A mightie Spyre, whose toppe dothe pierce the skie,
> An ivie greene imbraceth rounde about …
> And while it standes, the same doth bloome on highe,
> But when it shrinkes, the ivie standes in dowt:
> > The Piller great, our gratious Princes is:
> > The braunche, the Churche: whoe speakes unto hir this.

> I, that of late with stormes was almost spente,
> And brused sore with Tirants bluddie bloes,
> Whome fore, and sworde, with persecution rent,
> Am nowe sett free, and overlooke my foes,
> > And whiles thow raingst, oh most renowned Queene
> > By this supporte my blossome shall bee greene.

Another example of stylised imagery appears on the embroidered *Ahasuerus and Esther* panel (cat.11). The stylised clouds and the rainbow dropping rain could represent forgiveness and redemption. This motif was also used on embroidered garments, such as a late sixteenth-century smock in the Whitworth Art Gallery.

There is some evidence that sampler designs could be read symbolically but, again, interpreting the possible meanings of such motifs is hazardous without corroborating evidence. When Queen Elizabeth visited the Dowager Lady Russell at Bisham, her two daughters, Bess and Ann, welcomed her dressed as shepherdesses and embroidering samplers. One sampler showed men's tongues, symbolising lies, and the follies of the gods. The other showed virgin goddesses surrounded by the Queen's flowers – roses, pansies and eglantine. However, most samplers were working textiles intended as a personal collection of needlework patterns for use on clothing and domestic linen as well being the first stage of developing essential feminine embroidery skills. Barnabe Riche's 1581 story *Of Phylotus and Emilia* illustrates this domestic use of samplers very clearly:

> ...then she might seke out her examplers [samplers], and to peruse whiche worke
> would doe beste in a ruffe, whiche in a gorget, whiche in a sleeve, which in a quaife [coif],
> whiche in a caule [caul], which in a handkercheef...

These patterns could derive from a master sampler belonging to a teacher or from pattern books. The Venetian Federico Vinciolo published a highly popular pattern book that was constantly reprinted. Publishers shamelessly copied from each other. Patterns from Johann Sibmacher's *Modelbuch* printed in Nuremberg appeared in John Taylor's pattern book *The Needle's Excellency* printed in London. This non-pictorial design tradition is represented in the Ashmolean collection by the samplers and by the forehead cloth and coifs. These personal items of headgear have carefully balanced designs containing with stylised flowers. Although the designs themselves combine controlled symmetry with a lively sense of movement, there is rarely any attempt to relate the design to the actual shape of the coifs. Similar patterns appeared on a variety of decorative objects, including Elizabethan and Jacobean wallpapers. The lining of a deedbox in the Ashmolean is made from such wallpaper. The design appears to include a graphic representation of stitches suggesting that the designer was copying from embroidery rather than the other way round.

Animals, Birds & Flowers

Designers, including pattern drawers and embroiderers, had access to numerous printed sources depicting animals, birds, insects, plants and flowers. Designers and embroiderers used natural history compilations, reflecting contemporary interest in classifying the world, but they also had access to a range of publications which were deliberately intended as design sources. This helps to explain the repeated use of similar motifs on many embroideries. An almost identical frog in rushes appears on the Ashmolean's embroideries of *Abraham entertaining the Angels* (cat.4) and *The Proclamation of Solomon* (cat.9). However, it is often difficult to identify embroidered examples with a specific printed source, particularly as engravers tended to borrow freely from each other. Some motifs can be more clearly linked with sources as they are more identifiable. The monkey eating fruit in the Ashmolean's *Adam and Eve* (cat.1) is a fairly common motif; a comparable monkey appears in Francis Delaram's 1620 *Booke of Flowers Fruicts Beasts Birds and Flies*. This book retained its popularity throughout the century and was listed in Stent's 1662 catalogue. Similar designs for the crouching lion and the rabbit seen in both versions of *Adam and Eve* can be found in *The Book of Beasts*. A similar fish to the one shown half in and half out of the water appears in Hollar's *A New Boock of Flowers & Fishes*. The violets in the central foreground of the *Man wrestling with a Lion* (cat.13) are similar to those in Overton's plate showing 'slips' of fruit and flowers. The large version of *The Sacrifice of Isaac* (cat.6) demonstrates the complexity of trying to assign embroidered motifs to a specific source. Thomas Johnson's 1630 *Booke of Beast, Birds, Flowers, Fruits, Flies, and Wormes* contains a large flat multi-petalled flower similar to the flower worked in the border of this embroidery. Johnson also includes some flowers derived from Crispin van de Passe's 1614 *Hortus Floridus* which contains an iris comparable to that on the embroidery. Either book could have been used as the design source. The exotic birds looking over their shoulders bear some resemblance to an eagle in the *Hortus Floridus*. This appears on the same page as a drawing of some pears, suggesting that both the birds and the fruit could have been derived from the same source. Crispin van de Passe enlivened his designs with small insects and beetles. They have some resemblance to those in the border of the pastoral embroidery but it is not easy to distinguish one beetle from another unless they are worked with very distinctive features.

Real or Fantastical?

Not all the creatures are realistic. A similar unicorn to that worked on one of the Ashmolean's *Adam and Eve* (cat.2) embroideries appears in *A Book of Four-Footed Beasts* (c.1664). Stent's 1662 *A New Book of all Sorts of Beasts* was designed to help children learn to read and includes a mermaid, holding a mirror and combing her hair. Young girls embroidering their Old Testament stories could have had early familiarity with such fantastical creatures. Nevertheless, some aspects of these embroideries may be more representational than initially seems likely. The verses *The Virgin's Pattern*, written to honour Susanna Perwich after her early death, may hold a clue here:

cat.2, detail showing unicorn

Pictures of men, birds, beasts & flowers
When Leisure serv'd at idle hours
All this so rarely to the life
As if there were a kind of strife
Twixt Art and Nature: trees of fruit
With leaves, boughs, branches, body, root,
She made to grow in Winter time
Ripe to the eye'

The realism of Susanna's embroidery is being praised here. This is an unexpected virtue for twenty–first–century viewers looking at a tree bearing multiple types of fruit. However, it is important to remember that contemporary gardeners were famed for their success in grafting different fruiting branches onto a single tree stock – so such trees could be the depiction of the latest horticultural advance. The elaborate fountains and waterspouts may also reflect fashionable gardening styles.

cat.11, detail, Ahasuerus under a canopy

Lucy Harrison described her husband's ceremonial equipment when he was Charles II's Ambassador to Portugal. This included a 'crimson velvet cloth of state, fringed and laced with gold, with a chair, a footstool and cushions, and four other stools of the same, with a Persian carpet to lay under them'. Compare this with the formal presentation of Solomon in both *The Proclamation of Solomon* (cat.9) and *Solomon and the Queen of Sheba* (cat.10). In the latter, Solomon is shown standing under a ceremonial floral patterned canopy or cloth of state, decorated with pearls, and supported on marbled columns with a backcloth embroidered to represent a zigzag woven fabric. Such canopies, called 'cloths of state' were reserved for the highest-ranking persons. Bartolomeus van der Helst's 1640s painting of Maria Stuart, daughter of Charles I, (Rijksmuseum, Amsterdam) shows her seated on a silver throne on an exotic carpet under a velvet canopy. Edmund Harrison was the official Embroiderer to James I & VI and Charles I. When he re-applied for his post after the 1660 Restoration, Harrison produced Charles I's finest cloth of state and a pearl-embroidered carpet which he had hidden during the Commonwealth. This carpet sounds remarkably similar to the fringed floral carpet on which Solomon stands to receive Sheba which was also ornamented with pearls, although most are now missing. Unlike the fabrics of the women's gowns in this embroidery, the flowers here do not form a definite pattern and may represent floral tributes rather than a woven design. The canopies in *Ahasuerus and Esther* (cat.11) are carefully detailed with backcloths in different 'fabric' patterns and 'fringes'. The central canopy has a stylised floral design and a backcloth in a small diagonal repeating design, suggesting a woven fabric such as cut velvet. Esther's banquet takes place under a canopy bearing the Dyers' Company coat of arms with a backcloth patterned in small circles. The canopy over Ahasuerus's bed is worked in narrow stripes separated by leaf-like forms and has a backcloth in a toothed stripe, again suggesting a woven fabric. The presentation of monarchs in the embroideries would thus seem to echo their presentation in court life.

Clothing and fabrics seem to have been depicted in loving detail, using a rich variety of techniques and luxurious materials. Some of the dress fabrics have small repeating floral patterns, possibly suggesting brocaded silk. Biblical figures are often shown in antique robes whereas Kings may be shown wearing classicised versions of military dress. Female figures may be shown in fashionable dress although allegorical figures are more likely to be shown in stylised dress to emphasise their symbolic status. The figure of *Charity* (cat.14) is a case in point here. Her dress has been changed from the classical robes shown in the engraving to a dress and tunic exposing her breasts. Such exposure, in real life, would normally only have been permissible in specific situations, for example a court masque. Interestingly, some of the female figures are shown fully dressed but with their breasts clearly visible beneath their clothes. Small details, such as shoes and hair, may help suggest a possible date range. However, a later embroiderer could easily copy earlier styles so caution is necessary before dress, shoe or hair styles are used as aids to dating these embroideries.

Embroidery Stitches & Materials

Seventeenth-century taste appears to have valued ingenuity in the creation of embroidered images more than originality in their selection. Hannah Woolley boasted that 'after fourteen years old, I never was taught one stitch and most what I do now, is all from my own fancy' and set out her abilities with admirable clarity:

> I can work well all manner of works which is to be wrought with a Needle, also Transparent works, Shell-work, Moss-work, also cutting of Prints … All kinds of Beugle [bead]-works, upon wyers or otherwise…

Frustratingly, she gives few technical details. Stitch names change and it is not always easy to identify stitches such as those listed by John Taylor in his poem *The Praise of the Needle* with the flat, pile and raised work seen on the embroideries:

> For Tent-worke, Raised-worke, Laid-worke, Frost-worke, Net-worke,
> Most curious Purles, or rare Italian Cut-worke,
> Fine Ferne-stitch, Finny-stitch, New-stitch, and Chain-stitch,
> Brave Bred-stitch, Fisher-stitch, Irish-stitch, and Queen-stitch,
> The Spanish-stitch, Rosemary-stitch, and Mew-stitch,
> The smarting Whip-stitch, Back-stitch, and the Cros-stitch:

This stress on 'fancy' is supported by Randle Holme's slightly despairing comment in his *Academy of Armory* (published in 1688). As Deputy King of Arms, Holmes details technical descriptions used in the material world in order to translate them appropriately into heraldic terms. His list of 'The School Mistris Terms of Art for All her ways of sowing' includes stitches familiar from Taylor's poem but he concludes:

> all of which are several sorts and manners of Worke wrought by the Needle with Silk … Purles, Wyres, etc. which cannot be described.

Detached needlepoint stitches, whether used with fine linen thread for miniature lace collars or in coloured silks for the padded forms of human figures and animals, were capable of many variations. Great skill was used in the creation of the raised work features, which were often padded with ravellings of silk sewing threads. Hands and faces are sometimes found in carved wood, often covered with silk satin fabric.

Silk threads ranged from smooth glossy threads to the highly twisted threads which were used for depicting hair, manes and rocks. Metal threads include wrapped threads, consisting of strips of silver-gilt and silver, wrapped around silk cores. Flat metal strips, called 'plate', were also used. Coiled metal threads, the 'purl' mentioned by Randle Holmes, were themselves sometimes wrapped in fine silk thread. More complex metal threads could be made of combinations of plate, wire and silk, all coiled around each other. Sequins, glass beads, semi-precious stones, hair or peacocks' feathers were used to highlight details and create a lavish and glittering effect.

Raised work caterpillar worked in detached needlepoint stitch using silk thread and peacock feathers from cat.9, *The Proclamation of Solomon.*

Raised work mermaid from cat.9, *The Proclamation of Solomon,* with twisted silk threads, metal threads, pearls and coral beads.

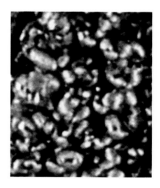

Complex metal thread from cat.4, *Abraham entertaining the Angels.*

The Proclamation of Solomon (cat.9) demonstrates the subtlety with which stitches and threads could be combined. The garments are carefully detailed to indicate the relative status of the characters. Solomon's coronation cloak has an 'ermine' lining while his doublet has metal thread loops and small pearl 'buttons'. Tufts of thread and one remaining pearl suggest the lattice-patterned breeches once had overall pearl decoration. His hose is worked in plaited Gobelin stitches in alternating directions giving a knitted effect. Solomon's needlepoint collar and cuffs are more ornate than those of the priest, Zadok. These are in turn more ornate than those of the prophet Nathan. The carnation and parrot have been constructed from sections of separately worked detached needlepoint, sometimes wired, to create three-dimensional or free-standing forms. The applied needlepoint sections making up the leopard and lion have been padded and stitched to create life-like contours. Both the lion's mane and the mermaid's tail are made from coils of a spring-like metal thread wrapped in silk. The remains of bundles of actual hair can be seen amongst the silk-covered coiled wire thread forming the maid's hair. Peacock feathers, now degraded, highlight the butterfly, winged insect and caterpillar. The sculptural rocks, embellished with pearls, coral or cornelian beads, are formed from twisted coils of metal thread. The waterspout is made from wired detached needlepoint. The stream of water pouring out of it consists of freestanding metal threads. Mica windows bring a touch of realism to the palace although the mica in the mermaid's mirror has been replaced with another later but still transparent material.

These embroideries survive as the physical witness to the lives and interests of the girls and young woman who spent such time and skill in their creation.

European Textiles in the Ashmolean Museum

The Department of Western Art in the Ashmolean Museum holds a number of other woven or embroidered textiles.

Two small tapestry panels, probably from the late sixteenth or early seventeenth century, were made at William Sheldon's tapestry factory in Worcestershire. One shows the apocryphal story of *The Stoning of the Elders*, focusing on the punishment of the judges who had secretly spied on Susanna while she was bathing. The other depicts the New Testament parable *The Return of the Prodigal Son* (Luke 15: 11-32). The two large 'Diana' tapestries are from the Paris workshop of Frans van den Planken and Marc de Comans, two Flemish weavers. *Latona and her Children* illustrates the episode when Latona, who had borne the twins Diana and Apollo to Jupiter, was escaping the anger of Juno, Jupiter's wife. During her flight, Latona tried to drink some water from a lake. The peasants who prevented her were changed into frogs as a punishment. The second tapestry shows *The Death of Orion*. Jealous of his sister's love for Orion, Apollo tricked Diana into shooting an arrow at her lover while he was swimming. These tapestries were commissioned at the time of the 1625 wedding of Marie de Bourbon and the Prince of Savoy-Carignan and show their coat of arms. The Gobelins tapestry *Combat des Animaux* (Battle of the Animals) is from a series known as *Teinture des Anciennes Indes*, woven from the early eighteenth century onwards. This tapestry may have been presented by the King of France to the Emperor of China. The other two tapestries are from the mid-seventeenth century Brussels workshop of Jan Raes the Elder and show scenes from the lives of the Old Testament ruler King David and the medieval hero Godefroy de Bouillon.

Amongst the embroidered pieces are three pieces of medieval *opus anglicanum* (English work) depicting various saints in architectural settings. These are English orphrey panels which would originally have been stitched onto church vestments but have been removed and remounted. Other pieces include a sixteenth– or seventeenth–century embroidered valence which is likely to be French or Scottish. This was probably intended for domestic furnishings and shows a formal garden with three ladies, representing the virtues Hope, Charity and Justice, guiding a bearded man. The large seventeenth–century needlework hanging *A Musical Party* shows musicians in an ornate garden setting and is probably Spanish or Portuguese. A finely worked embroidery showing the story of tragic story of *Jephthah and his daughter* (Judges 11: 29–39) is possibly Italian, following a design by Andrea Mantegna.

Acknowledgements

I would like to thank Timothy Wilson, Catherine Whistler and their colleagues at the Ashmolean Museum, Nell Hoare MBE, Dinah Eastop and Julia Bennett (Textile Conservation Centre, University of Southampton) and Linda Newington and her colleagues (University of Southampton Library, Winchester Campus) for their generous support and help. I am indebted to Nancy Graves Cabot for her pioneering identifications of printed sources, Santina Levey for her observations on the needlework flowers, Hilary L.Turner for sharing her research into the Sheldon tapestries and Lynda Hadden of The Sampler Guild for comments on the samplers. I would also like to thank C.E.A.Cheesman, Rouge Dragon Pursuivant, College of Arms for advice on heraldic identifications. I wish to acknowledge grants from the Arts & Humanities Research Board, the British Academy, the Millennium Commission Sharing Museum Skills Scheme and the University of Southampton for financial support during the research leave which enabled this work to be undertaken. My greatest thanks are due to Jo Walton for introducing me to the Ashmolean textile collection.

A note on the catalogue

Unless otherwise specified, all the embroideries were bequeathed by J.Francis Mallett in 1947. As Mallett's collection consists mainly of embroideries with biblical subjects, the catalogue entries have been arranged broadly in the order of the bible stories followed by the allegorical and secular pictures, samplers, costume accessories and the novelties. Embroideries given by other donors have been included at the appropriate point in this sequence. A copy of this introduction giving full details for all references has been deposited in the Department of Western Art and copies are available on request. Dimensions have been taken at the maximum extent and are given in millimetres in the order height, width and depth.

1   The Temptation of Adam and Eve

First half of seventeenth century
279mm x 322mm   WA1947.191.307

According to the biblical story, Adam and Eve were the first man and woman created by God. This embroidery depicts the moment when Eve, who has succumbed to the serpent and eaten an apple from the tree of the knowledge of good and evil, is now tempting Adam (Genesis 3: 6). The design is unusually symmetrical. The tree of knowledge, with the serpent twined in the branches, is in the centre with Adam and Eve on either side. The right cloud band contains a sun, representing day. This is flanked by two winged cherubs and below a motif which may be the all-seeing eye of God. The left cloud band contains a moon, representing night, with cherubs and stars. Unusually, the sun is above Eve while the moon, traditionally associated with the feminine, is above Adam. Other similar embroideries exist, such as a cushion in the Colonial Williamsburg Foundation. This suggests a common print source existed, possibly a biblical illustration.

Contemporary proverbs often compared women with animals. Monkeys were considered to represent women's foolish behaviour which may explain their appearance here and on the Colonial Williamsburg embroidery.

The embroidery is worked on plain weave linen fabric with a selvage containing two blue stripes on the left side. The right edge has been cut while the top and bottom edges have rolled hems. The embroiderer has used the margins for practise, working experimental designs for the cherubs' eyes. The silvery sky is worked in plaited Gobelin stitch, a lavish use of metal wrapped thread. Elsewhere, the piece is worked in fine tent stitch in silk threads. The large butterfly contains the remains of an iridescent filament which may be peacock feathers. The tree, leaves and insects are carefully shaded but the interpretation of Adam and Eve's bodies and the water is stiff and clumsy.

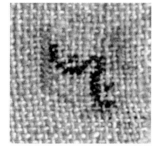

Cherub's head worked in the border.

2   The Temptation of Adam and Eve

Mid seventeenth century
570mm x 585mm   WA 1947.191.308

Here Eve is shown tempting Adam with the apple that the serpent has enticed her to eat from the tree of knowledge (Genesis 3: 6). Night is indicated by a moon and stars while day is suggested by a sun. The figures of Adam and Eve are highly distinctive: Adam is shown almost crouching while Eve is standing with her left leg crossed in front of her right. Another, although less sophisticated embroidery, shows Adam and Eve in a similar pose. This suggests a common printed source which could possibly be Bernard Salomon's illustration in Claude Paradin's 1553 verse version of the Bible.

Embroideries of Adam and Eve often include both real and imaginary creatures. The exotic elephant and the legendary unicorn depicted here could be symbolic as well as decorative. Elephants were symbols of modesty and chastity, especially that of Adam and Eve before the temptation. Unicorns symbolised purity and chastity and could also represent Christ or the Virgin Mary. Together, they could be intended to underline the moral message of the story and hint at the theological link between the temptation of Adam and Eve and Christ's redemption of fallen mankind.

The embroidery is worked on a single piece of plain weave linen with selvages at the top and bottom. Tent stitch is used throughout, often with considerable subtlety. Careful colour gradations create a dimensional effect. Metal threads highlight special features. The sun and moon are worked using a wrapped metal thread in Gobelin stitch with plaited Gobelin stitch for the sun's rays. The pond's waves are in silver wrapped metal thread. The waterspout is worked in laid and couched wrapped metal thread. Six metal spangles, secured with a wrapped metal thread, remain from the original eight which formed the ring of stars around the moon. The under-drawing is visible where the embroiderer left the inked outlines unworked or where, as on the snake, the silk thread has fallen out.

Opposite bottom: Bernard Salomon's illustration of *The Temptation of Adam & Eve* in Claude Paradin's verse picture book of the Bible, *Quadrins de la Bible*, translated into English as *The true and lyuely historyke purtreatures of the Vvoll Bible* (Lyon 1553).

GENESE III.

Le faus Serpent, à tromper entendu,
Vint finement, à Eue se renger,
Et tourna tant, que du Fruit defendu:
Elle, & Adam, se prindrent à manger.

3   The Finding of Moses in the Nile

Dated 1629
430mm x 540mm   WA 1947.191.306

The earliest dated embroidery in the collection, this shows the finding of Moses in the River Nile (Exodus 2: 5). Pharaoh had ordered all the newborn Israelite boys to be killed but Moses's mother hid him in a cradle in the Nile, where he was watched over by his sister Miriam. Pharaoh's daughter discovered the baby and brought Moses up as her son. Moses later led his people out of slavery.

No printed source for this unusual embroidery has yet been identified. Miriam is shown holding Moses, wrapped in swaddling bands, while Pharaoh's daughter stands on the far bank of the Nile. The personification of the Nile as a half-naked crowned woman appears to be unique. However, a different version of *The Finding of Moses* (Metropolitan Museum of Art, New York) includes a mermaid who may be intended to represent the Nile. The coats of arms are probably those of the Manson or Nanson family with those of the Bernham or Brenham family, suggesting that the embroidery commemorates a marriage. Whitney's *A Choice of Emblems* (1685) includes a picture of an obelisk with a climbing plant which is similar to those in the side borders. Whitney's verse celebrates political faithfulness but the image could also be appropriate for marriage. Several interpretations are thus possible. The embroidery could reflect concerns about political loyalties and, possibly, the royal succession or personal issues such as marriage and the birth and safe upbringing of male heirs. A 1644 embroidery of *The Finding of Moses* at Parham Park, traditionally considered to be a christening cushion, reinforces the latter interpretation.

The dazzling sun created with a variety of metal threads.

The embroidery is worked on plain weave linen in Gobelin stitch using a silvery metal thread for the lustrous background, overspun silk threads for textured areas and tent or long and short stitch in silk threads elsewhere. Two different types of linen fabrics act as support patches for the cherubs and the figures. *Solomon and the Queen of Sheba* (cat.10) is the only other embroidery in this collection with similar patches.

4   Abraham entertaining the angels

Second half of seventeenth century
430mm x 460mm   WA 1947.191.314

Abraham is shown entertaining three angels who, to his astonishment, foretell the birth of Isaac to his barren wife Sarah (Genesis 18: 1-6). The careful scale and perspective reflect the close relationship between the embroidery and its source, a print from Gerard de Jode's 1585 collection of biblical illustrations. The pose of Abraham and the angels is almost identical in both but either the designer or the embroiderer found the perspective of the porch difficult. Some features have changed significantly. Instead of buildings, the upper left corner shows Sarah's maid Hagar with Ishmael, her son by Abraham. Two lavish jugs now lie in the prominent dish. The landscape has been enlivened by the addition of a countryman walking near a watermill and a pond with a waterspout, rocks, coral, frog and fish. Several versions of embroideries based on this print survive. One example in the Victoria & Albert Museum includes the story of Abraham sacrificing Isaac although the large dish is without the jugs.

The story of Isaac's birth was a popular seventeenth-century subject, reflecting concern over the duty of wives and issues of succession and inheritance. John Shaw's 1642 sermon makes an explicit link between Sarah's unexpected pregnancy and the complexity of contemporary political events: '... who would have said that Sarah should give suck; so who would have said, three yeares agoe, that we should have a parliament, a trienniall, parliament, and that not to be broken up by mutual consent?'

The embroidery is mainly tent and Gobelin stitch worked on plain weave linen. Three edges are hemmed while the left side is a selvage with one blue warp. French knots or laid and couched metal threads, sometimes padded, highlight details such as the jugs and wings. Stem and overcast stitches form the eyes, small couched strips of metal plate the windows. Metal thread braid stitch over pink silk threads frame the image. Rococo stitch, braid stitch and an area of tent stitch are practised in the margins.

The raised work jugs created using different types of metal threads.

Opposite bottom: *Abraham entertaining the Angels* from Gerard de Jode's compilation *Thesaurus Sacrarum Historiarum Veteris Testamenti*, 1585.

PARITVRAM SARAM NVNCIANT ABRAHÆ ANGELI HOSPITES, SARÆQVE RIDENTI PROMISSIONIS VERBA RETERÀT

De Heer verscheen Abram, soo dat dry Mannen quamen
Door syn Huys, daer hy sat: Hy noodse met Eere,
Sy aten met hem broodt: ende Seyden te samen

Sara sal eenen Zoon hebben, om dese tijdt;
Sy Jacob achter de Deur, hoorende dit, gewaer,
Om dat Sy was zeer Oudt, en Abram hoogh van dagen

5   Abraham's dismissal of Hagar

Mid seventeenth century
288mm x 383mm   WA 1947.191.312

Before Abraham's wife Sarah gave birth to Isaac, she
thought herself barren. In order to ensure that Abraham
had heirs, Sarah encouraged him to take her maid Hagar as
his mistress. Hagar gave birth to Ishmael. Later, when Sarah
saw Ishmael mocking Isaac, the late born but rightful heir,
she asked Abraham to dismiss Hagar. Abraham sent Hagar
into the wilderness, providing her with bread and a bottle
of water. Desperate after her wanderings, Hagar prayed not
to see Ishmael die from thirst. An angel appeared,
prophesying Ishmael's future, and revealed a well to Hagar
(Genesis 16 & 21: 9-21).

This embroidery closely follows the print in Gerard de
Jode's *Thesaurus Sacrarum Historiarum Veteris Testamenti*
although there are interesting differences. Hagar's clothes are
little changed but her hairstyle is more fashionable. Rather
than chiding the two quarrelling boys in an open doorway,
Sarah is shown with Isaac under a floral canopy. The
landscape is now filled with buildings, animals, trees and a
pond complete with a waterspout, rocks, coral, fish and a frog
in reeds. This print was very popular with embroiderers and
a version in the Burrell Collection demonstrates the freedom
with which it could be interpreted. Although almost identical
in overall design, details such as the women's clothes differ
while a mermaid with comb and mirror floats in the pond.

Sarah was seen as a role model for women, praised in
N H's *Ladies Dictionary* as 'an obedient, Virtuous and
beautiful Woman.' However, it is impossible to tell whether
the story was intended to inculcate moral behaviour in
women or simply to provide a pleasurable opportunity for
embroidery.

The embroidery is worked in silk tent stitch on a single
piece of undyed linen. Laid and couched stitching has been
used for mouths and noses but the eyes are worked in two
colours in more random couching, adding animation to the
faces. Some of the embroidery has been lost, particularly on
the left side. The narrow braid edging may be a later addition.

Opposite bottom: *Abraham's Dismissal of Hagar* from Gerard de Jode's 1585 compilation *Thesaurus Sacrarum Historiarum Veteris Testamenti.*

CVM PVERO ISMAELE PROCVL DIMITTITVR HAGAR, QVEM SARA HÆREDEM NOLVIT ESSE SVVM.

Sara Verfocht Abram, dat hy uyt wilde Iagen   Hy deede, en gaf haer Broot, met Water on dit pas,
Hagar, met haren Soon, Want hy moetwillich was.   Sy weeck in de Woeftyn, daerstiet sy mengen treden.
Ghât vermaande Abram te doen syn Wyfs behaghen.   Want t'kindt ftorf fchier van dorft, Maer d'Engel hielp haer
                                                      Iaen.

6   The Sacrifice of Isaac

Dated 167(3)
Maker's initials I (E or Y)
445mm x 555mm

WA. OA.414
source unrecorded

The date and initials are worked in pearls on the padded bosses of the elaborate cartouche. Although the pearls making up the second initial and the last number are missing, their impressions allow the date to be read as 167(3) and the initials as I and E or Y.

This embroidery shows a critical episode in Abraham's life when he demonstrated his obedience to God by offering his son Isaac as a sacrifice, before an angel pointed out a ram as an alternative (Genesis 22: 1-14). Abraham's willing offering was considered to foreshadow God's sacrifice of his son, Christ. For the young girls embroidering the story, the moral may have been simpler – the virtues of obedience to parental authority and of faith in divine love. This story attracted many seventeenth-century artists.

At least thirty embroideries on this theme survive. Identifying a direct source is not easy as the images are very similar. This embroidery seems closest to van Panderen's engraving, which was also used by Elizabeth Illingworth for her 1613 embroidered book cover (Victoria & Albert Museum). The engraving was also the source for book illustrations, such as the title page of John Downame's 1622 *A Guide to Godlyness*, and for interior decorations, including an overmantel in a house in Oxford High Street.

The ground fabric is cream silk satin with two selvages containing three green stripes. The dramatic central scene is highly dimensional. The figures are made from applied and padded sections of detached needlepoint. Isaac's head is almost completely free-standing padded silk satin. Abraham's sword hand is carved wood, probably once covered with a woven fabric. His cloak is wired to give the effect of movement. The long and short stitches used for the altar, wood and urn are worked over thicker threads or wire. The cartouche is formed of a padded roll of detached needlepoint supported on a silk-wrapped parchment

Opposite bottom: Egbert van Panderen's engraving of *The Sacrifice of Isaac*, c.1600 after Pieter de Jode.

or leather strip. The sculptural birds in the border are padded or wired detached needlepoint sections. Their padded heads and multi-sectioned wings are free-standing, applied over 'shadows' worked in long and short stitch. The large fruits are made from detached needlepoint on carved wooden forms. The grassy knoll beneath the lion is worked in cut-pile stitches while that below the leopard is made from overspun silk threads. Mica, a transparent mineral, is used to highlight the palace windows. Contemporary roll-topped pins secure the gateposts, fruit, birds' wings and Abraham's cloak.

Opposite: Detail of Abraham and Isaac. Note Abraham's hand in carved wood which may once have been covered in fabric.

7 Scenes from the life of Abraham

pre 1665
Maker: possibly Miss Bluitt, later Mrs Payne
297mm x 265mm x 185mm   WA 1947.191.315

Abraham was a symbol for unconditional faith and a model for kings and rulers (Genesis 16: 21 & 24). However, for schoolgirls the essential message of the story was probably the importance of marriage and the proper behaviour of women, as seen in the lives of Sarah, Hagar and Rebecca. The note accompanying the box reads:

> The Cabinet was made by my Mother's Grandmother who was educated at Hackney School after the Plague in London all the young Ladies works were ~~burnt~~ destroyed that they were about at that time, she left school soon after, therefore this was made that vis before 1665 – The cockade was what was worn at the Coronation of George Ist done Sr Samul (?) Bluitts Daughter who afterwards married Mr Payne Mr Payne Daughter married Mr Samual Cotes of Peckham it was given by her Aunt H Cotes– to Ann Brookes.

A further comment, in different handwriting, records that 'Ann Brooke's mother Christiana Brookes was daughter of Samuel Cotes of Peckham'. Although slightly ambiguous, this suggests the box was made by Anne Brookes' great grandmother, Mrs Payne, as a schoolgirl. The creation of such boxes was the culmination of a girl's needlework education. The embroidered panels were sent away to be mounted up which may account for the rather unsympathetic placing of the key plates and the silver handles. The bottom compartment contains four drawers. These are covered in pink velvet while doors are covered inside with embossed pink silk.

Detail showing the construction of Sarah's face and hair.

The lid shows Sarah with her son Isaac. On the left door, Abraham is dismissing Hagar, clasping her son Ishmael by the hand. The right door depicts Hagar kneeling in prayer with the miraculous well behind her and Ishmael lying faint beneath a tree. On the right side, Abraham is instructing his steward Eliezer to go abroad to find a wife for Isaac. The back shows Rebecca, Isaac's future

Opposite top: The front doors of the box showing *Abraham's dismissal of Hagar* and *Hagar praying in the wilderness*.
bottom: Anne Brookes' note.

The Cabinet was made by my Mothers Grandmother who was educated at Hackney School after the Plague in London all the Young ladies Works were burnt destroyed that they wear about at that time, she left school soon after, therefore this was made that very before 1665 — The Cockade was what was Worn at the Corination of Geurge 1st done by Sr Samul Bluitts Daughter — who afterwards married Mr Payne Mr Payne Daughter married Mr Saml Coter of Peckham it was given by her Aunt H Coter to wife. She is giving Eliezer water from a well while camels drink from a nearby trough. On the left side a fashionably dressed couple, presumably Isaac and Rebecca, stand near a young boy holding a camel.

There is no known print source for the design of Sarah standing in a tent although it occurs frequently, e.g. cat.5. Some of the embroidery designs relate to engravings in Gerard de Jode's collection: Rebecca's pose as she gives Eliezier water from an elegant pitcher is very similar to the de Jode engraving. However, this rather stilted version of the story of Hagar has changed considerably from the print. Ishmael now stands between Abraham and Hagar. She carries a basket of food instead of holding bread in her looped-up skirts and has no water bottle. The positions of Hagar and Ishmael in the wilderness have been reversed.

The young embroiderer demonstrated remarkable inventiveness and skill although the quality of the work varies. No attempt has been made to create a coherent landscape or any perspective in the raised work on the lid top, tiers and doors. In contrast, the tent stitch pictures on the sides and back appear more fluent and assured with more developed landscapes and some sense of depth. The raised work areas are worked on a silk satin ground. The sculptural figures, which stand on grassy mounds made in cut pile stitches or laid overspun silk, are constructed from sections of detached needlepoint padded with fragments of silk thread. Padded appliqué silk satin, satin stitch or detached needlepoint with embroidered features has been used to create their faces. Thick wire wrapped with silk forms their hands. A foundation of what may be human hair lies under the finer silk wrapped coiled metal wire forming their hair. Sarah's dress is tent stitch in a small floral design; the left section is a later, painted replacement. Collars and cuffs are made from applied sections of detached needlepoint lace in fine linen thread. Sarah's tent is detached needlepoint with a fringe made from needlepoint and silk floss. Peacock feather remains can be seen in the raised work caterpillar on the lid. The three tent stitch panels are enlivened with pearls. Ink underdrawing is visible.

Opposite top: The back of the box showing Rebecca giving the water to Eliezer, Abraham's servant.
bottom: Detail of running dog in padded detached needlepoint.

43

8   David & Bathsheba

Dated 1661 or 1681
Maker's initials S C
368mm x 480mm   WA 1947.191.310

Adultery and murder may seem an unsuitable subject for schoolgirl embroiderers but the seventeenth-century artists and writers who presented the story of David's seduction of Bathsheba, the wife of Uriah the Hittite, took this as an opportunity to moralize about appropriate behaviour while also depicting female charms (II Samuel 11: 2-27 & 12: 1-15). This embroidery shows King David on his palace balcony watching a maidservant carry his letter to Bathsheba. She is bathing in a pool with an elaborate lion head fountain which bears the date 1661 or 1681 and the initials S C. In the bottom left, David, knowing Bathsheba is to bear his child, questions Uriah. He had hoped to conceal their adultery but Uriah, recalled from the war, refuses to sleep indoors with Bathsheba while his comrades are on the battlefield. David therefore instructs his servant Joab to engineer Uriah's death in battle, depicted in the upper right corner. The lower right corner shows the prophet Nathan admonishing David. Nathan tells David the parable of a poor man's sheep, illustrated by the depiction of the countryman, sheep and dog.

Several embroideries based on Gerard de Jode's engravings survive. Four of these engravings are combined here. Although the poses of the embroidered figures follow the engravings quite closely, there are some significant changes. The winged horse fountain, peacock, statues and Italianate buildings are all missing. The leafy arbour has become a floral arch. The exchanges between David and Uriah and David and Nathan no longer take place in elegant townscapes but are located in front of small round topped tents while the battlefield has been reduced to Uriah's death scene.

Bathing outside is not as unrealistic as it might appear, even in the English climate. Bolsover Castle still has a Jacobean cold bath with an elaborate Venus fountain which originally spouted water over bathers seated in niches.

Opposite bottom: *Bathsheba Bathing* from Gerard de Jode's 1585 compilation *Thesaurus Sacrarum Historiarium Veteris Testamenti*.

Dum lauat et recreat gelido sua flumine membra Bersabee regis litera missa datur. 2. Reg. cap. 11.

Gerardus de Iode
excudebat

45

This embroidery is worked in exceptionally fine tent stitch on undyed linen. Some areas, such as Uriah's helmet and breastplate, seem to have been left deliberately unworked so the underdrawing is still visible. Elsewhere, underdrawing is visible where the embroidery thread has degraded. Other areas, such as Bathsheba's mirror, seem to have later ink or overpainting, presumably intended to restore the visual impact of the original outlines.

Above: Detail of Uriah's death in battle.
Opposite top: *David and Uriah* from from Gerard de Jode's 1585 compilation *Thesaurus Sacrarum Historiarium Veteris Testamenti.*.
middle: *Uriah's Death in Battle* from the same source.
bottom: *The Prophet Nathan admonishing David for his Sins* from the same source.

Rex rogat Uriam de bello, mittit et illi, Addita nectareis vina iocosa cibis. 2. Reg cap. 11.

Hoc cadit in belli conflictu, positus ante Urias, regis fidus amicus erat. 2. Reg cap. 11.

Regi adest domini iussu propheta Nathanus. Monstrat adultery, cædis et esse reum. 2. Reg cap. 12.

9   The Proclamation of Solomon

Mid to late seventeenth century
354mm x 475 mm   WA 1947.191.313

This panel shows the unusual subject of the young Solomon
being proclaimed King of Israel (I Kings 1: 30-35). No
printed source has yet been identified. Following the dying
King David's wishes, Zadok the Priest and the prophet
Nathan, shown holding the book of the Law, present
Solomon to the people. Solomon is crowned and holding a
sceptre. Benaiah, the Captain of the King's Guard, and
Bathsheba (Solomon's mother) and her maid stand a little
way off. A mermaid, holding a mirror and comb, floats in
an elaborate pool, flanked by a seated lion and leopard.
Although the main figures are in scale, the hilly landscape in
which they stand is filled with outsize flowers and insects.
The textiles are remarkably detailed and the clothes are
subtly differentiated to indicate the figures' relative status.
Solomon's ceremonial canopy has marbled columns and a
zigzag striped backcloth, distorted at the top indicating
points of attachment.

Detail showing the construction
of Solomon's face and hair.

The panel is mainly embroidered in subtly shaded tent
stitch on linen. The faces and hands are made from
appliquéd silk satin with eyes worked in stem stitch and a
thicker couched thread. Hair has been created using a
variety of methods. Solomon's is lightly padded long and
short stitch whereas Nathan's is laid and couched silk
wrapped wire thread. The maid's is worked with bundles of
hair, possibly human, couched amongst the coiled silk
wrapped wire thread. Other stitches and threads are used to
highlight details. The lion's mane and the mermaid's tail are
made from coils of metal thread wrapped in silk. Peacock
feathers, now degraded, highlight the butterfly, winged
insect and caterpillar. The sculptural rocks, embellished with
pearls, coral or cornelian beads, are formed from twisted
coils of metal thread with a spout made from wired detached
needlepoint from which pours a stream of water made of
free-standing metal threads.

Cat.10 has some similarities of design, materials and
technique. It is intriguing to speculate whether the two
embroideries may be linked in some way.

49

10   Solomon & the Queen of Sheba

Mid to late seventeenth century
312mm x 468mm
Presented by C.M.D. Peters   WA 1994.142

The Queen of Sheba travelled to visit King Solomon because she had heard of his 'wisdom and prosperity' (1 Kings 10: 1-13 & II Chronicles 9: 1-12). Some legends suggest Solomon and Sheba had a child, and the Ethiopian royal dynasty traces its ancestry back to this illustrious couple. As well as depicting an heroic woman, the embroidery could refer to ideal monarchs or marriages, linking wisdom and wealth. The numerous embroideries showing Solomon receiving the Queen have different print sources. Gerard de Jode's dramatic version shows Sheba in a contorted pose, kneeling before Solomon. Although this engraving is not a direct source for this embroidery, the ornate urn is a link between the two. Remaining pearls and tufts of threads suggest the embroidered urn once had a handle, making it more similar to the urn in the print.

This embroidery is worked on a piece of hemmed linen. The raised work includes appliqué and padded silk satin and detached needlepoint, wired to create free-standing petals or wings. Some techniques are remarkably similar to those on cat.9, particularly the embroidery of the eyes using contrasting thickness of silk thread around solid black pupils. Both use a modified Gobelin stitch for the men's stockings and similar methods for embroidering hair. The waterspout is a roll, possibly of parchment, encased in a needlepoint mesh of metal threads while the gushing water is made from various metal threads. Peacock feather remains are visible on some insects.

Small patches of a different fabric on the back are puzzling; they bear the inked design of a mermaid, similar to that on the front. These could be original support patches, such as those on cat.3, or later repairs. If original, they raise interesting questions. Did the pattern drawer offer a design on linen as well as satin to enable experimental stitching? Was the embroiderer perfecting her designs on a practice fabric which she then used to stabilise areas of dense stitching? Lack of comparative examples makes any conclusions here difficult.

Detail of head; note the bundles of hair.

Opposite bottom left: Reverse side of *Solomon and the Queen of Sheba* showing the patch with the mermaid design.
Bottom right: the patch rotated 90°.

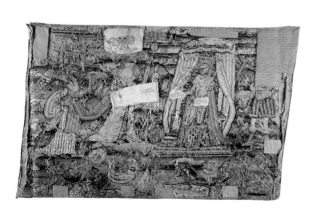
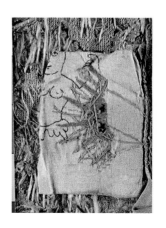

11   Ahasuerus & Esther

Dated 1654
Maker's initials A H
412mm x 550mm   WA 1947.191.309

The Old Testament's *Book of Esther* tells a complicated story of male intrigue and female bravery. King Ahasuerus, encouraged by Haman, is threatening the Jews but is unaware that Esther, his second wife, is Jewish. Haman plots against Esther's Uncle Mordecai who had earlier saved the King. Risking her life, Esther invites Ahasuerus and Haman to a banquet and pleads for her people. Haman's plotting is exposed and he is hung on the gibbet he had prepared for Mordecai. The Feast of Purim commemorates Esther's bravery in saving the Jews.

The various stages of this story are shown set in a hilly landscape crowded with animals. Ahasuerus is shown at the centre under formal canopy. This is dated 16/54 on the marbled pillars and has the initials A H on the pinnacle. The King extends his sceptre to Esther, indicating that she may step onto his ceremonial carpet. In the upper right, Ahasuerus is shown lying sleepless in bed, being read the 'Book of the Law' through which he learns of Mordecai's great loyalty. A small scene in the upper centre shows Mordecai being honoured by riding the King's horse. Esther's banquet is on the upper left side under a canopy bearing the Dyers' Company coat of arms. Haman's execution by hanging is in the top right corner. The pool, complete with mermaid, contains a fountain which has an indistinct scene of a King with a harpist, possibly David playing to Saul (I Samuel 16: 23). The fountain is topped by a small winged figure of Old Father Time carrying a sickle and a winged chalice containing a host (communion wafer).

A H's embroidery draws in part on Gerard de Jode's print in the *Thesaurus Sacrarum Historiarum Veteris Testamenti*. The addition of the unusual images such as the chalice and host, the King and harpist, and the lion with the sinister bone suggest some specific meaning was intended. The lion in the Burrell Collection's version is seated in front of a pile of clean bones. Both embroiderers

Opposite bottom: *Esther's Banquet* from Gerard de Jode's compilation *Thesaurus Sacrarum Historiarum Veteris Testamenti*, 1585; the pleat in the table cloth is also clearly visible in the embroidery.

Accusatur Haman, reginaque crimina pandit Jairidæ structam sustinuitque crucem.   Ester. cap. 7.

could have been using the story of the brave, yet obedient, Queen who spoke out in defence of her people to make a religious or political point, which could have been supporting either establishment or minority viewpoints.

The embroidery is worked on linen in fine tent stitch using silk threads with knot or split stitches for the eyes and buttons. The crowns are formed from laid and couched metal threads crowns while the King's chain is an applied plait of metal thread

Above: The fountain ornamented with the enthroned King and harpist and the winged figure of Father Time carrying a sickle and winged chalice with a host. *Opposite*: Detail. Note the ceremonial carpet.

55

12 Isaac, Samson & Saul

Mid seventeenth century
179mm x 315mm   WA 1947.191.318

This book cover is divided into three sections. The front shows *Abraham's Sacrifice of Isaac* (Genesis 22: 2-14), the spine *Samson Triumphant* (Judges 15: 14-17) and the back *Saul's Conversion on the Road to Damascus* (Acts 9: 3-4). Depictions of Samson and Saul, later St Paul, are rare in embroidery of this period and images from the New Testament are particularly unusual.

The embroidery is a mix of pictorial scenes and formal motifs. The horizon line, cloud bands and sun's rays link the front, spine and back visually. The depiction of the sacrifice of Isaac focuses on the dramatic moment when the angel seizes Abraham's sword. This design follows an engraving by Egbert van Panderen although the image has been reversed. Samson was famous for his great strength. In the violent episode evoked here, he had been captured by the Philistines but burst his bonds and killed thousands of his captors with the jawbone of an ass. He is carrying the jawbone, standing between two panels containing stylised flowers with snails and insects. The back shows the transforming moment when Saul had his blinding conversion from persecutor of Christians to committed believer. A large scroll worked in gold and silver metal threads has the remains of the words spoken by the Lord: 'Saul, Saul, why persecutest thou me?' This design may be a much simplified version of Bernard Salomon's print, which is also a possible source for the painted cloths showing the life of St Paul at Hardwick Hall.

The cover is a slightly uneven oblong piece of fabric, hemmed on all edges. The paper lining has a watermark of a vase and the initials 'PP' under a crescent moon. The embroidery is worked mainly in flat stitching with some raised elements. The embroiderer has used a large number of different metal threads to create an effect of concentrated richness in details such as the angel's wings, the urn, and the rock formation. Some rust stained holes suggest that nails were used in an earlier mounting method. There are repair stitches in yellow and red threads.

Detail of the spine showing a carnation surrounded by snails and small insects.

13 Man with a Lion in a Landscape with two couples

Second half of seventeenth century
314mm x 401mm   WA 1947.191.311

This finely detailed embroidery shows a man with a lion between two couples in a hilly landscape crossed by a meandering stream. The sophisticated use of pictorial space creates a sense of depth while the figures' fluttering mantles and the rippling water give a sense of animation and movement. Several identifications of the main figure are possible. He could be the classical hero Hercules fighting the Nemean lion, a popular subject during the sixteenth and seventeenth centuries. Tapestries showing the Labours of Hercules were amongst those recalled by the parliament for use by Cromwell. Alternatively, he could be Samson wrestling with the Lion of Timnoth (Judges 14: 5-9). However, the image could also be intended to read symbolically. Cesare Ripa's *Iconologia* depicts self-control or magnanimity as a man wrestling with a lion and makes an explicit link between this virtue and Hercules. An unfinished embroidery in the Burrell Collection shows a similar man wrestling with a lion, although the image is reversed.

The two couples are intriguing. Images of couples appear in seventeenth-century books on marriage and collections of ballads on the themes of love, betrothal and marriage. It is not clear whether the couples here, whose differences in age and dress seem deliberate, relate to such themes or, just possibly, represent different religious or political groups. Could there be a link between the symbolic depiction of the virtue of self-control and advice given to couples on behaviour in marriage?

Opposite bottom: *Self-control* from Cesare Ripa's *Iconologia*, 1645.

59

The smaller background figures may simply be intended as customary features of a pastoral scene rather than having any symbolic meaning. They include a shepherd piping to his sheep and a countrywoman balancing a basket, possibly containing flowers, on her head. She could be a dairy maid, a rural stereotype often associated with courtship. A tiny figure, carrying a large burden, crosses the furthest bridge.

The embroidery is worked in fine tent stitch with subtle colour graduations on linen. Details such as the eyes are highlighted using split stitches, with overcast stitch for the pupils. The thatch and windows of the building in the upper left corner are ornamented with half long cross stitch. The remains of underdrawing and black embroidery indicate the original edge of the design. The surrounding fabric has been partly cut or worn back to this outline.

Opposite: Detail showing the figure on the bridge near the palace and watermill.

14 Charity standing in a landscape

Mid to late seventeenth century
312mm x 425mm   WA 1975.13
Presented by Professor J. Tyrwhitt

The allegorical figure of Charity is a relatively unusual subject for English embroideries of this period. Charity is one of the Seven Virtues and personifies non-romantic love and kindness. This design, showing her bare-breasted with children, is close to an engraving by Crispin de Passe the elder. There are some differences: Charity has one less child while her traditional attribute of a flaming heart is held by the child on her right rather than by the one in her arms. The naked children have been clothed in stylised tunics but Charity's classical robes have been altered to a robe and short tunic which exposes her breasts. This indicates her allegorical status rather representing fashionable dress.

There is little sense of perspective; individual motifs seem to have been more important than creating an overall coherent picture. The foreground is totally covered with smooth stitching, except for a pool with a waterspout and elaborate rocks worked in many different metal threads and decorated with beads of faceted glass or coral. The gigantic glittering raised work fish is covered with small sequins. Single stitched lines are used to outline the rolling hills, leaving the creamy satin ground visible. The three-dimensional animals in the border might be intended to have a symbolic meaning. The unicorn suggests purity and chastity. The camel could represent Asia but might also reflect excitement caused by the first visit of a dromedary to England. In March 1652/3, Daniel Fleming, an Oxford student, paid 4d 'for ye sight of ye Dromoidary'. The edges of the border are filled with a symmetrically balanced design of alternating insects, birds and exotic flowers, whose long wavy stems create an interlinked pattern

The subject of Charity was clearly an improving theme for young girls. The uneven, although lively, nature of the embroidery suggests that this was more of a technical than a moral exercise and may be unfinished. Some underdrawing is still visible although it is likely that elements, such as the children's faces, were intended to be left unembroidered.

The elaborate fish in the pond with waves and rocks created using metal threads.

Opposite bottom: *Charity* by Crispin van de Passe the elder after Maarten de Vos.

15   A Pastoral scene

Mid to late seventeenth century
332mm x 455mm   WA 1954.90
Presented by Dr. G. J. S. Mouncey-Atkinson

Seventeenth-century poets and artists often depicted the
countryside as a place of innocence where love could
flourish away from the pressures of urban life. Court ladies
and fashionable beauties were depicted as shepherdesses,
including the King's mistresses Barbara Villiers and Nell
Gwyn. This panel combines a typical pastoral scene, set
inside an ornamented oval frame, with a deep border of
isolated flowers, birds, animals and insects. An elegantly
dressed shepherd and shepherdess are seated under a
stylised tree. She is accompanied by three sheep while a
spotted dog dances to the bagpipes played by the shepherd.
The two buildings have sophisticated towers, spires and
carefully detailed roofs and windows. Fragments of mica, a
transparent mineral, remain in the windows. Most of this
scene is worked in flat stitches with French knots and
basket stitch to add texture. The creamy silk satin ground
fabric has been left unembroidered to form the sky. The
ornate raised work cartouche was created by laying silk
threads in carefully graduated tones over thicker linen
threads. The fleur-de-lys and the stylised groups of leaves
are worked in long and short stitch and French knots and
have an inlay of brown, possibly once black, silk. This
fabric is now degrading.

The deep border also leaves the ground fabric exposed.
Each corner is filled with a large flower 'slip'. These were
embroidered separately on a linen fabric using tent or
rococo stitch, then cut out and applied to the satin fabric.
The edges are carefully concealed under black laid and
couched threads. Two exotic birds, similar to those on cat.6,
are worked in smooth long and short stitches. The same
stitches were used for the miniature scene of a lion, leopard
and small pond below the cartouche. Tightly curled silk
threads were used to create the lion's mane. The familiar
motif of a running dog chasing a hare is worked in flat
stitches. The lively caterpillars, beetles and a butterfly are all
worked in flat stitches highlighted with knots.

16   Samplers

Dated 1660. Maker Mary Parker
930mm x 162mm   WA 1947.191.322
Dated 1699. Maker Mary Parker
763mm x 212 mm   WA 1947.191.321
Dated 1667. Maker Suzannah Connington
830mmx 195mm   WA 1990.41
                    Bequeathed by J Buxton

These three samplers demonstrate the variety of designs
and techniques which could be contained within the band
sampler format. The intriguing pair of samplers bearing
the same name, Mary Parker, are over thirty years apart
while Suzannah Connington's sampler, dated 1667, falls
between the two. Mallett acquired the two Mary Parker
samplers from a Norfolk family and it is tempting to
speculate that they were made by relations, possibly an
aunt and her niece.

The 1660 Mary Parker sampler is in intricate
whitework, creating a lace-like effect. Techniques include
cut work, where the ground fabric has been removed, and
pulled work, where the threads making up the fabric have
been manipulated to create patterns, together with
needlepoint and needlewoven fillings. There are twenty
different bands containing a variety of complex repeating
geometric and floral motifs. The 1699 sampler is signed
MARY PARKER MAY THE 9 ANNO DOMINI 1699
IN THE 11 YEAR OF HER AGE. It has fourteen
different bands in pink, green and blue silk threads. The
stylised motifs, including a thistle and knot motif and
strawberries, roses and acorns, are alternated or inverted to
form repeating patterns. These are worked in a variety of
flat stitches including cross-stitch, featherstitch, fly stitch
and running stitch with some detached needlepoint. The
three small figures holding sprigs, now called 'boxers'
because of their fighting stance, are thought to have
originated in Continental designs of couples exchanging
gifts. Suzannah Connington's 1667 sampler includes bands
of coloured and whitework embroidery and a central
section of 'spot' motifs. These independent motifs include
birds, a rabbit, dog and deer as well as peapods, stylised

Opposite: Sampler, Suzannah
Connington, 1667.

flowers, leaf motifs and a hearts and a small hand holding a strawberry. Her simple but effective stitches include running and backstitch with some raised and pulled work.

Designs could be taken from the many printed pattern books which contained floral, bird, animal and geometric designs. Pupils could also purchase samplers from their teachers in order to copy their designs. A group of samplers made around Ipswich between 1691 and 1710 are associated with one teacher called Juda or Judeth Hayle. Several motifs on the 1699 sampler, such as the thistle and knot, appear on samplers in the Cooper-Hewitt Museum, New York, and the Fitzwilliam Museum. The acorn motif used by three of Judeth Hayle's pupils - Ann Holwell, Sarah Bantoft and Mary Groome - also appears on the 1699 Mary Parker sampler. This raises the intriguing possibility that the Parker samplers might have some link with the Ipswich sampler group.

Inscription from Mary Parker's
sampler, 1660.

Inscription from Mary Parker's
sampler, 1699.

Opposite left: Sampler, Mary
Parker, 1660.
right: Sampler, Mary Parker, 1699.

17   Glove Gauntlets

Early seventeenth century
Gauntlet A (pink peapod) 125mm x 345mm
Gauntlet B (blue peapod) 130mm x 345mm

WA 1947.191.317

This pair of square tabbed gauntlets, or cuffs, would originally have been mounted on a pair of gloves. Gloves were fashionable accessories for both men and women and were status symbols as much as protective clothing. They were often given as expensive gifts which also indicated respect and loyalty. The pair of white kid gloves associated with Elizabeth I's 1566 visit to Oxford have decorative embroidered gauntlets. James I was presented with a pair of gloves costing £6 when he visited Oxford University in 1605. These had a 'turnover [gauntlet] wrought with purl [metal thread]'. Ineffectual attempts were made to restrict the wearing of more lavish gloves. However, a visiting Italian noted in 1618: 'All wear very costly gloves. This fashion is so universal that even the porters wear them very ostentatiously.'

These gauntlets are probably the only example of professional work in the Mallett donation. The gloves on which they were mounted were probably a soft leather such as lamb or doeskin. Each gauntlet is embroidered on linen with a central vertical seam presumably lined up with the side seam of the gloves.

The motifs are identical on both gauntlets although the colours vary. The repeating motifs include a pea plant and pods, complete with peas, a honeysuckle and a thistle with a butterfly. The base contains a carnation, a bunch of grapes and a stylised rose. The flowers are partly worked in tent stitch with bold shading while stems and veins are highlighted with coiled metal threads. Other parts of the flowers, buds and the grapes are in detached needlepoint, giving a dimensional effect which is further enhanced by some padding. The thistle flowers are made from tufts of floss silk, creating a realistic texture. The motifs are further ornamented with sequins. The ground fabric is covered by Gobelin stitch worked in metal thread. The underdrawing is visible beneath some of the applied sections.

71

18 Two Coifs & a Forehead Cloth

Coif with peapod, roses, carnations & pomegranate
design
218mm x 395mm   WA 1947.191.318
Additional section
42mm x 195mm
Coif with roses, borage & foxgloves design
210mm x 390mm   WA 1947.191.319
Forehead Cloth
Late sixteenth to early seventeenth century
365mm x 256mm   WA 1947.191.320

These are indoor head coverings worn by women in the late
sixteenth and early seventeenth centuries. Forehead cloths
had different names including cross-cloths, crosses or
crossets. A 1689 Dutch/English dictionary describes them
as 'a woman's brow-piece; so called, because it is put cross
the forehead.' Opinions vary as to whether they were worn
with the point forwards or backwards. Forehead cloths
appear to have been particularly associated with illness. In
1617 Fynes Moryson noted 'Many weare such crosse-
clothes or forehead clothes as our women use when they are
sicke.' Some women embroidered their own headgear. The
1620s Howard Accounts record the payment of 12d for
'drawing 2 coifs of my lady's and for the cloth'. Ellen Field's
1619/20 inventory values her 'crascloathes [crosscloths]
with other wearing leenen [linen]' at ten shillings.

   Some matching coifs and forehead cloths survive but
these pieces do not relate to each other. One coif has a
double scroll design containing ten different stylised
flowers including roses, borage and foxgloves. The other has
a more linear double scroll design in which rows of peapods
and roses alternate with rows of carnations and
pomegranates. This coif has a small strip of a different
fabric, probably a later addition, attached to the top seam
which is embroidered in a modified Greek key design.

Opposite top: Coif with peapod,
roses, carnations & pomegranate
design.
bottom: Coif with roses, borage
& foxgloves design.

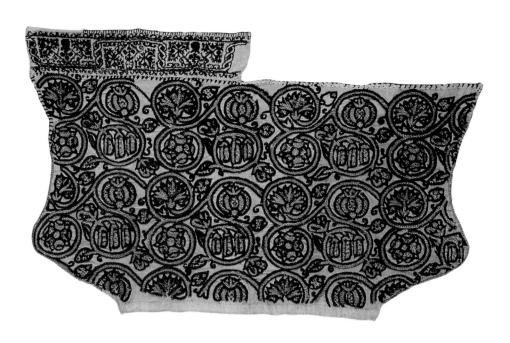

Both are worked in black silk thread and metal threads in a variety of flat and filling stitches and now have the top seam unstitched. Originally, this longer edge would have been sewn up and the curved side edges would have covered the ears. Turnings at the neck edge form carriers for drawstrings to pull the coif close. Although their basic shape is very similar, the curved sides have been created very differently. The peapod and roses coif has neat hemmed seams and the metal braid stitch edging has been placed to decorate the edges most visible in wear. The curved sides on the roses and borage coif have deep irregular turnings which have been slashed so they lie flat. The full length of these side edges is trimmed with a metal thread lace decorated with sequins.

The forehead cloth is a single piece of fabric, cut on the bias and hemmed on all sides. The design of interlaced leaves on stems with scrolls and hanging star motifs is worked in double running stitch and open buttonhole stitch. Some of the petals and spaces are filled in with metal thread basket weave stitch while others are decorated with metal sequins. Sequins are also stitched at intervals along the scrolls. The underdrawing is visible in the right hand corner.

Opposite: Forehead cloth.

19   Frog Purse

Seventeenth century
60mm x 75mm x 15mm   WA 1947.191.324

This charming purse is made in the form of a frog with four
legs and a drawstring opening at the mouth. Such little
purses are too small and fragile to be functional for coins
and may have been made as personal gifts to hold small
perfume sachets or herbs. Frogs were clearly a popular
motif and several embroideries here include them, often
sitting in a clump of reeds, such as cat.4, cat.5 and cat.13.
A sinister hag in Ben Jonson's 1609 *Masque of Queens* uses
an actual frog skin to make a purse to hold a fly:

> The blood of frog and the bone in his back
> I have been getting and made of his skin
> A purset to keep Sir Cranion [a fly] in

Several frog purses survive, all slightly different. The
Museum of London's frog purse has limbs which are covered
in needlework in contrast to the wrapped wire used here.

   Two firm sections, possibly leather, with some padding
form the base of the purse. These are covered with a green
silk plain weave fabric. A continuous network of needlepoint stitches is worked over this fabric using a metal thread
composed of a silk thread wrapped around with a fine wire.
A mottled appearance has been created on the bottom
section by laying down little patches of green silk floss
between the silk and needleworked mesh. A spring-like
golden metal thread surrounds the eyes which are made
from green and black glass beads. The same thread also
decorates the upper section and edges. An inner pleated bag
of cream silk, attached only at the hinge and at the 'mouth'
opening, forms the actual purse. The two base sections are
connected at the frog's 'tail' where the hinge is decorated
with more of the spring-like metal thread. Thick wire bound
around with the wire wrapped threads for part of their
length forms the limbs and four-fingered 'hands'. The
'finger tips' are wrapped in silk threads. The fine drawstring
cord is made from five silk and two wrapped metal threads.
The hinge has stitched repair work

Close up showing construction
and metal threads.

76

20 Nut tape measure

Seventeenth century
90mm x 70mm x 20mm   WA 1947.191.325

Decorative tape measures were popular novelties in the seventeenth century. This example uses a nutmeg as its base. Another similar nut measure (National Museums of Scotland) is also covered in a mesh of metal and silk threads and has two long paper tapes with these verses:

> The God above vouchsafeth store. To him in fault
> that prayeth therefore: But for his quifts you thankless
> run: Their wealth shall waste as wax in Sunn.
> Aske what thou wilt and though shalt have; if though in
> Christ yu same do crave: For Christ thy mediator
> sees when tough to him doest fall knees.

Mary Hannay's 1687 measure, previously in the collection of Sir Percival Griffiths, was in the form of a three-dimensional rose and butterfly. The inscription on the tape suggests this was a gift:

> Take this small present at my hand
> Who am your servant to command.

Another measure has a central silk bound wire with silk tassels and a small pod containing two strips of parchment. The verse suggests this was a love token:

> Mr Grine I have sent you this Leter to Remember me
> when this you See Except this Gieft tho it be Small you
> have my heart with hand and all. Elizabeth Beard 1684

The Ashmolean's measure has a mesh of detached needlepoint worked in a metal wrapped thread and silk thread at the top and bottom of the nut. This is linked by four narrow strips of an interlaced braid stitch worked in silk thread. Two of these are decorated with two tassels comprising a central ball, two pear-shaped tassels and three smaller bobbles with silk tufts. The parchment strip, unmarked as was normal until the eighteenth century, has a worked bobble so it can be pulled out easily. Rotating the central spool of heavy wire returns the tape into the nut. This is bent into a loop at the top which is bound in silk thread. It opens up into two separate wires at the bottom which are decorated with two pear-shaped tassels, each with three little bobbles with silk tufts. The pear shaped tassels may have a core, possibly of paper. One of the smaller bobbles from the central tassels is missing.

Opposite: Close-up showing the construction and metal threads.

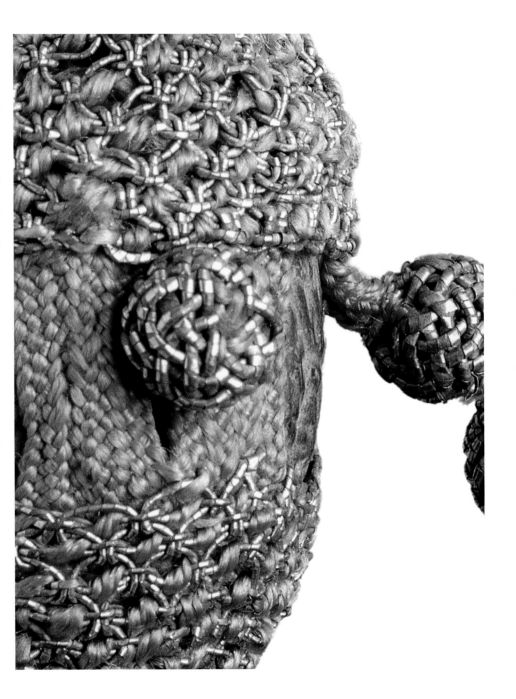

21   Three Needlework Flowers

Strawberries
100mm x 70mm x 2mm   WA 1947.191.323.1
Pansies
80mm x 80mm x 15mm   WA 1947.191.323.2
Marigold or sunflower
130mm x 90mm x 10mm   WA 1947.191.323.3

Seventeenth or nineteenth century

These delightful miniatures present an intriguing problem.
They could be seventeenth-century 'favours' or love tokens
but the technique suggests they could equally have been
made in the nineteenth century.

In their book *Domestic Embroidery* (1926), Seligman &
Hughes argued that the flowers seen in sixteenth- and
seventeenth-century portraits might be made 'in gold and
silver wire, cleverly twisted, bent and curled into quite
recognisable blossoms.' Although portraits do show flowers
and fruits being worn, such as the pansy, strawberries and
fern worn by Elizabeth I in her 1590 portrait in Jesus
College, Oxford, it is often hard to tell whether these are
real or artificial. Contemporary references suggest
needlework flowers could be used in a variety of ways, both
symbolic and decorative. In 1617, the pupils of the Ladies
Hall, an elite school, performed a masque for Queen Anne.
The Queen's goddaughters presented her with
needleworked gifts of an acorn and rosemary, referring to
her initials 'A R'. Hannah Woolley's 1674 book describes
how to decorate a plain picture frame using shells, mother-
of-pearl, coral and amber as well as 'little flowers of several
colours [made] upon round pieces of cards, with small satin
ribbon, and fasten some wire for the stalks.' This is clearly
a different technique from that of the Ashmolean's favours
but does show the interest in making three-dimensional
flowers. An embroidered box containing a needlepoint
carnation and bunch of strawberries survives at the
National Museums of Scotland.

In contrast, the basic technique for the Ashmolean favours is interlaced stitching. The use of this stitch is unexpected as seventeenth-century embroiderers tended to use variations of detached needlepoint lace stitches for such structures. The strawberry leaves are sections of interlaced stitches, joined together to form three points. The flowers are also interlaced work on small silk covered cores, possibly wood, surrounded by coils of metal thread. The padded strawberries are stitched together with either a cream or greenish thread to give a speckled effect. The pansies and marigold are made using the same technique. Dye analysis might resolve this dating issue but, paradoxically, the good condition of these pieces precludes sampling.

Close-up of the pansy showing construction techniques.

22   Embroidered Panel

Early to mid seventeenth century
147mm x 248mm

WA 1958.57.38
Bequeathed by A G B Russell

This small embroidered oblong is probably professional rather than domestic work. The ornate vase holds a single large upright rose surrounded by symmetrically balanced flowers including a pansy, honeysuckle, borage and carnation. Two winged caterpillars march along the stems of the honeysuckle flowers. Foxgloves occupy the lower edge together with parts of two snail shells. The motif of a vase with flowers was clearly popular. Thomas Trevelyon, a Cornishman who was possibly involved in the textile trade, created two unique manuscript collections of illustrations and designs. His 1608 *Miscellany* and 1616 *Great Book* include some drawings of vases of flowers which are comparable to this embroidery. An embroidered box in the National Museums of Scotland features a vase design which is also similar to a design in the *Miscellany*. Similar vases appear on an early seventeenth-century cushion cover in the Metropolitan Museum of Art, New York with birds, flowers and insects. Such vases also appear in late sixteenth- or early seventeenth-century wall paintings at Woodhouse Farm, Great Horkesley, Essex.

Close-up showing the detached needlepoint used for the vase.

The panel is worked in wool and silk threads on a single piece of undyed plain weave linen fabric. The background is covered with closely worked Gobelin stitch while the flowers are carefully shaded tent stitch. The vase has been created using a wrapped metal thread in a detached needlepoint stitch outlined by laid and couched twisted metal threads. This is an economical use of expensive metal thread as very little is wasted on the reverse, whereas the Gobelin and tent stitch cover both sides of the fabric. The two snail shells and other flowers are highlighted with long laid and couched threads. Sparkle is added by the small metal sequins (many now missing) which are attached randomly over the embroidery. The slashed corners suggest the panel could possibly have been mounted on a support, possibly as a cushion pad. Nail holes indicate a previous display method. There are some losses, particularly along the bottom edge.

23   Embroidered bag

Nineteenth- or twentieth-century replica
80mm x 88mm   WA 1947.191.326

Little embroidered bags were used frequently as coin purses
or to hold perfume sachets in the sixteenth and seventeenth
centuries. Queen Elizabeth's skinner, Adam Bland, used
them to preserve her costly furs. The 1614 inventory of the
Earl of Northampton's possessions lists several including 'a
small white satten bagge embroidered with flies, worms,
and flowers in silks and golde'. This bag is made from a
single piece of silk fabric folded along the bottom edge
which is decorated with small tufts. It is lined in pink silk.
The drawstring is a tightly worked cord with ornamental
petal-like tags made using silk and metal threads. One face
depicts a standing woman with clasped hands. She is
flanked by small hillocks with two vines and flowering
plants. The second face shows a small bird perched in a
fruit tree surrounded by smaller trees, plants and birds.

The design and embroidery techniques raise doubts
about its date. Although superficially resembling motifs
found on sixteenth- and seventeenth-century embroideries,
the figure of the woman does not conform to the norm. No
attempt has been made to create detailed garments. There
is an unusual gap between the skirt and the bodice on the
right side. The bird and tree are closer to the design of
earlier embroideries but the spindly vines, flowers and
scrolling outlines, presumably intended to suggest clouds,
are atypical. The embroidery methods are not typical or are
fairly crude, such as the padded laid stitching used for the
grapes. The use of different coloured couching silks to
create details such as the sleeves, the skirt and the fruit is
unusual. However, some features are more typical, such as
the basket stitch forming some of the little hillocks. The
bag is in good condition which means that taking thread
samples for dye analysis to resolve the dating question is not
straightforward. The visual evidence suggests that this is
probably a nineteenth or twentieth-century replica based
on careful study of original pieces and using comparable
materials.

Stitch Definitions

Back stitch

Created by repeatedly bringing the needle up from under the fabric a little way from the starting point and then re-inserting it again at the beginning, thus creating a 'back' stitch.

Braid stitch

A surface stitch in which the thread is looped around the needle before securing it, thus creating a braid-like effect.

Chain stitch

A small loop made by winding the thread around the needle which is then secured by a small stitch worked in the same spot. This is then repeated to form a 'chain'.

Cross stitch

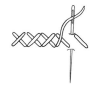

This stitch is usually worked by making a slanting stitch in one direction and then working back along the row making the slanting stitch in the opposite direction. When worked on canvas this may be called Gros Point.

Double running stitch

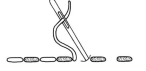

This is a running stitch worked in two passes, firstly from left to right and secondly from right to left (or *vice versa*) in the same place. The second line of stitching fills in the gaps left by the first. It is identical on both sides and gives the effect of a continous line of stitching. This is sometimes called Holbein stitch.

Feather stitch

The thread is worked in a series of loops each held down by each other and worked alternately in right and left directions. This is sometimes called 'plumage' stitch.

Fly stitch

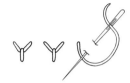

A series of single chain stitches worked independently.

French knots

These are used as filling stitches and consist of a knot made by wrapping the thread firmly around the needle and then securing it with a twist to the ground fabric.

Gobelin stitch

Small diagonal stitches worked over one vertical and two horizontal threads; worked in horizontal rows. In Plaited Gobelin stitch the rows overlap each other to produce a plaited or woven effect.

Irish stitch

Straight stitches worked in a zigzag formation. This is sometimes called Florentine work.

| Laid & couched stitches |  | A thread is anchored to the fabric by another thread using a couching stitch. This stitch is often used to secure expensive metal threads. |

Laid & couched stitches

A thread is anchored to the fabric by another thread using a couching stitch. This stitch is often used to secure expensive metal threads.

Long & short stitch

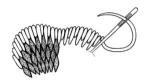

A variant of satin stitch, in which the first row consists of satin stitches of differing length and the second row is of satin stitches of the same length. These two alternating rows are continued until the desired area is completely covered.

Needlelace / Needlepoint

Generic terms for a wide variety of lace stitches made using a continuous thread and needle, often on a parchment foundation, rather than using bobbins on a pillow. This is a very flexible stitch and can be used to create a lace which is very open or a much tighter, fabric-like effect.

Rococo stitch

A canvas-work stitch in which several groups of stitches are worked in alternate squares, giving a 'pulled' work effect. This is sometimes called Queen stitch

Running stitch

The simplest stitch, in which the needle makes straight stitches of equal length.

Satin stitch

A filling stitch in which the thread is carried right across the area to be covered and then returns underneath the fabric to near the previous stitch's starting point to make the first stitch.

Stem stitch

A slanted stitch consisting of one long forward stitch and one short stitch taken backwards close to the previous stitch. This gives a slightly twisted effect

Tent stitch

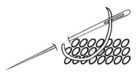

Small diagonal stitches worked over one vertical and one horizontal thread. It is often worked in a diagonal direction. This is sometimes called Petit Point.

Uncut and Cut pile stitch

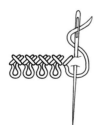

A secure loop is created on a foundation of diagonal stitches. The loop which may be left uncut for 'Uncut pile stitch' or cut to give a tufted effect for 'Cut pile stitch'. This is sometimes called velvet stitch.

These definitions are based on Mary Thomas's *Dictionary of Embroidery Stitches*.

Glossary

Appliqué — A separate fabric which is cut out and attached to the main ground fabric of an embroidery

Cartouche — An elaborate frame which may be oblong or oval and often has a scroll-like outline

Mica — A transparent mineral often used in a single sheet to give the impression of glass in mirrors and windows

Orphrey — Decorative band, often embroidered, applied to ecclesiastical vestments such as copes and chasubles

Plain weave — A fabric in which the warp and weft interlock at right angles in a repeated sequence of over one thread, under one thread. It is sometimes called tabby weave

Selvage — The long side edges of a piece of woven fabric which may have additional, sometimes thicker or different coloured warp threads to give additional strength

Satin weave — A fabric in which the warp threads pass over five or seven wefts so as to give a smooth reflective surface

Slip — A term derived from gardening, this refers to separate embroidered or fabric motifs which are cut out and then applied to the main ground of an embroidery or a larger textile

Warp threads — These threads run the length of the loom and are interlaced by the weft threads so as to form different woven fabrics

Weft threads — These threads cross the width of the loom and interlace with the warp threads in different repeated patterns to form different woven fabrics

Other collections

Many museums and historic houses have collections of sixteenth- and seventeenth-century embroideries. The following are some of the major collections in England and America

Great Britain

The Burrell Collection, Glasgow

The Embroiderers' Guild, Hampton Court Palace, East Molesey, Surrey

The Fitzwilliam Museum, Cambridge

The Holburne Museum, Bath

The Lady Lever Art Gallery, Port Sunlight, Liverpool

The Museum of London, London

The Victoria & Albert Museum, London

The Whitworth Art Gallery, Manchester

USA

The Colonial Williamsburg Foundation, Colonial Williamsburg

The Cooper-Hewitt Museum, The Smithsonian Institution, New York

The Metropolitan Museum of Art, New York

The Museum of Fine Arts, Boston

Further reading

Arthur, L. 1995. *Embroidery 1600–1700 at the Burrell Collection*. London: Murray & Glasgow Museums.

Brooke, X. 1992. *The Lady Lever Art Gallery. Catalogue of Embroideries*. Stroud: Alan Sutton & National Galleries & Museums on Merseyside.

Hackenbroch, Y. 1960. *English and other Needlework Tapestries and Textiles in the Irwin Untermyer Collection*. London: Thames & Hudson.

Nevinson, J. 1938. *Catalogue of the English Domestic Embroidery of the Sixteenth & Seventeenth Centuries*. (Second edition 1950.) London: HMSO.

Parker, R. 1984. *The Subversive Stitch*. London: The Womens' Press.

Swain, M. 1986. *Figures on Fabric*. London: A & C Black.

Thomas, Mary. 1985. *Dictionary of Embroidery Stitches*. London: Hodder & Stoughton.

Wells-Cole, A. 1997. *Art and Decoration in Elizabethan and Jacobean England: the influence of Continental Prints*. London: Yale University Press.

Witt, C. (ed.) 2000. *Telling Tales with Threads*. Bath: Holburne Museum of Art.